Life's 2% Solution

PRAISE FOR *LIFE'S 2% SOLUTION* AND MARCIA HUGHES

"*Life's 2% Solution* offers a well-defined process complete with maps and recipes for individuals who are ready to develop their true selves. It provides guidance, which will strengthen leaders who must address the vast array of problems that challenge the 21st century. Some of us will work with the process to move backwards and strengthen areas where our development is incomplete; others will develop their 2% Solutions to fearlessly become more than they thought they could. With this clarity you can re-vision and effectively tackle the mega-problems that challenge our planet, people and productivity. Please get it, and get busy!"

—Don Edward Beck, Ph.D.
Co-founder, National Values Center, Denton, TX
Founder/CEO, The Spiral Dynamics Group, Inc.
Founder/President, Center for Human Emergence
Author of *Spiral Dynamics: Mastering Values, Leadership, and Change*

"*Life's 2% Solution* is an important tool for professionals working in today's corporate world. Why wait until your next vacation to come alive? Marcia Hughes offers a powerful route to connect to a more meaningful life. While your glow from a vacation may last a day or two, investing 30 minutes a day will allow your glow to shine for a lifetime."

—Mary Broesch
Vice President and Actuary
ING U.S. Financial Services

"Through *Life's 2% Solution*, Marcia Hughes offers her immense wisdom of engaging life in a playful and constructive manner. Marcia offers many invitations, through practical exercises, for the reader to embrace their own 'dance of life' through a pathway of elegant simplicity. This book is not for the feint-hearted as its focused application may change lives!!"

—Christopher Cooke
5 Deep GmbH, Switzerland

"As we search for meaning in our lives and a way to make a difference in the lives of others, Marcia Hughes shows us that it's not the quantity of our actions—2% to be exact—but the quality of them that helps us get there."

—Suzanne Kirk
FVP, Bank Operations
Commercial Federal Bank

"*Life's 2% Solution* is worth 100% of your attention. Comprehensive, sensible and readable, the book is a great blueprint for helping us keep our equilibrium while we tackle the tough issues that face us during the day. It reminds us that we need not relinquish our dreams despite the pragmatic realities of the day. And it reminds us that to be effective externally, we need to spend time with our inner selves. Marcia Hughes has contributed invaluably to those who are seeking to make the world a better place."

—Phil Goldsmith
Goldsmith Advisors
Former chief operating officer of the City of
Philadelphia and former chief executive officer of
the School District of Philadelphia

Life's 2% Solution

*Simple Steps to Achieve
Happiness and Balance*

Marcia Hughes

NICHOLAS BREALEY
PUBLISHING

BOSTON • LONDON

First published by Nicholas Brealey Publishing Company in 2006.

100 City Hall Plaza, Suite 501
Boston, MA 02108 USA
Tel + 617-523-3801
Fax: + 617-523-3708
www.nicholasbrealey.com

3-5 Spafield Street, Clerkenwell
London, EC1R 4QB, UK
Tel: +44-(0)-207-239-0360
Fax: +44-(0)-207-239-0370
www.nbrealey-books.com

Printed in the United States of America

10 09 08 07 06   1 2 3 4 5

ISBN-13: 978-1-85788-365-7
ISBN-10: 1-85788-365-9

Text design by Lisa Garbutt of Rara Avis Graphic Design

Library of Congress Cataloging-in-Publication Data
  Hughes, Marcia M.
    Life's 2% solution : simple steps to achieve happiness and balance /
  Marcia Hughes.
       p. cm.
    Includes bibliographical references (p. 245) and index.
    ISBN-13: 978-1-85788-365-7
    ISBN-10: 1-85788-365-9
    1. Self-actualization (Psychology) 2. Success—Psychological aspects.
  3. Life skills. I. Title: Life's two percent solution. II. Title.

    BF637.S4H84 2006
    650.1—dc22
                          2005033120

To Bob, to my wonderful family, and to all those who have so courageously sought a passionately meaningful life and have been willing to share their stories for this book and throughout my work.

CONTENTS

7/

Learning from Others: Pinpointing Your Personal 2% Solution   139

8/

Zap the Map: Integrate Your Mind, Body, and Soul   163

9/

The Authentic Leader: Your 2% Solution at Work   187

10/

Sing from Your Spirit: The Key to Self-Actualization   209

FOREWORD

What the world needs now is guidance in learning to live with the many gifts offered to us. A huge cry is rising in our fast-paced, hard-driven world—a cry from the soul that demands we connect to what is truly meaningful in our lives. Yet some feel overwhelmed, believing there is no opportunity for personal time. Today we know that to alleviate these problems, successful remedies must be insightful and to the point.

In *Life's 2% Solution*, Marcia Hughes creatively presents a practical approach to making a difference in your life. This approach requires only 2% of your time—30 minutes a day or 3½ hours a week. It is transformative and sharply focused on finding what she calls your "Esprit d'Core," the spirit at the core of your being. By following the steps, action plan, and exercises in *Life's 2% Solution*, you are guided to find your deep calling, bringing it to life and experiencing a significant shift in your world. You are more centered in dealing with challenges, and you are happier because you are bringing your purpose to life.

I know this 2% Process works as I have observed individuals develop 2% Projects in leadership groups for many years. When people are engaged with what truly matters, their lives shift. Marcia has taken the 2% Project and given it meat, bones, and longevity—developing a solution that has enduring benefits. She provides specific guidance for its implementation, then demonstrates the differences that occur by choosing a lifelong solution, not just a short-term project. She calls for a lifestyle that regularly invests 2% of your time in yourself. This is a simple, yet radical, approach.

My life's work has focused on understanding the brain—recognizing how thinking and behaving affects one another as depicted by the Emergenetics® Profile. Marcia's 10 steps to implementing a 2% Project taps into the dynamic connection between thinking and behaving.

When you search for your Esprit d'Core, you use all of your mental resources by choosing a specific project to focus your engagement for 30 minutes a day. This process strengthens and upgrades your behaviors. The combination of seeking, reflecting, and acting is the formula for transformation, which *Life's 2% Solution* guides you through with grace, wisdom, and humor.

I remember the day Marcia captured the phrase that depicted how she wanted to live, "passionate equilibrium." This phrase calls for living in a style that guides us to success with both happiness and balance. *Life's 2% Solution* is the culmination of Marcia's work and assists you in finding a passionate equilibrium in your life. This book aids businesses to motivate their employees and individuals to liberate their lives from the obstacles and clutter that block true purpose and fulfillment. Thank you, Marcia, for providing this great guidance! And to you, the reader, best wishes on finding the 2% that really matters.

—Geil Browning, Ph.D.
Founder/CEO, Emergenetics International
Author of *Emergenetics*: *Tap Into the New Science of Success*

ACKNOWLEDGMENTS

My greatest and deepest thanks goes to my life partner, James Terrell. Thank you for being a wonderful husband, business partner, and for your dedicated support of this project throughout its long birthing. Your editorial assistance, cheerfulness, and patience are central to this book's existence. I also wish to thank many other people: Marilyn Harding conducted many of the 2% interviews with grace and flare. Without your help, Marilyn, I don't know how this project could have happened. My nearby family, John, Mary, Ken, Don, Bill, and Shelly provided unfailing support. And to Julia, the best daughter I could ask for, thanks for cheerfully and frequently saying "Write your book, Mom!"

Thanks to my agent Michael Snell for believing in me and this work and for your watchful and patient eye as you guided this forming ship. Thanks to everyone at Nicholas Brealey Publishing— Patricia O'Hare, for voting for *Life's 2% Solution* and working on behalf of its success, my editor Erika Heilman for your good humor and consistent commitment, Chuck Dresner and Carmen Mitchell for your commitment to sales and publicity. Thanks also to O.C. O'Connell for your amazing and enthusiastic editing help and to Hawley Roddick for your early editorial help. My gratitude goes to Roger Green for your help with research, and Danielle Hughes, Sherrol Horner, and Beverly Swanson for your typing assistance. A special thanks to Geil Browning, Carol Hunter, and Tim Rouse, founders of the leadership groups Influence and Focus, for introducing me to title 2% Project and for your longtime support of this project. Thanks to the vibrant and loving Wisdom Community for your support and good cheer. My humble gratitude to the many who have conducted 2% Projects and are implementing your *Life's 2% Solution*—thanks to all of you and especially those who so graciously shared your stories. The names and other identifying criteria of the people referred to in the 2% in Motion stories have been changed to protect their privacy.

INTRODUCTION

That which is most important must never be at the mercy of that which is least important.

— Goethe

You have a major presentation to give. Your budget is due. Your boss anointed you the go-to person for every request that comes into your understaffed department. You have just been given a new plum project. Somehow, you meet all the external demands of your life. You manage to juggle till you drop and then wonder why you have a nagging sense of incompleteness despite all that you've accomplished. Your cup runneth over—right onto your freshly dry-cleaned suit.

Does this sound familiar? The little trade-offs you make to get things done accumulate and have an insidious way of leaching away your creativity, passion, and sense of fulfillment. Instead of feeling connected and contented, you feel stressed and out of balance. You'd really like the opportunity to find out whether less is more.

I've been there. I have run myself ragged thinking that if I just get this other thing out of the way, I'll have time to do something for myself—spend more time hiking in the beautiful Colorado Rockies where I live, explore new spiritual paths, or take tai chi lessons again. I'm thrilled to tell you that I've been able to do all these things and more—without the benefit of winning the lottery!

It truly *is* possible to become a more effective and engaged leader in your workplace and to live a richly textured life that brings you great fulfillment without chronic burnout. No, I'm not in the huckster business; this is not a "miraculous cure for whatever ails your life in 30 days xx / Life's 2% Solution

or your money back" kind of offer. It's also not a fairy-tale ending. You can't get there via a yellow brick road, a magic carpet, or a twitch of your nose.

Your *Life's 2% Solution* is the lifelong transformation that you will gain as you implement your *2% Project*—a simple, practical strategy that requires just a pinch of time and a whole lot of heart. Your 2% Solution can change your life dramatically, but only with your consent and participation. It guides you in discovering your inner passion and creativity simply by reallocating 2% of your time each week. By dedicating just 30 minutes a day (or an equivalent amount in bigger, weekly clusters) toward satisfying an inner yearning, you will transform your life. You will gain an inner sense of well-being, and most important, you will no longer be at the mercy of superficial routines competing for priority.

By giving yourself the gift of spending 2% of your time intentionally devoted to what you truly love through a well-tested process called the 2% Solution, you will enjoy profound rewards. You will leave behind a fragmented life that pulls you in too many directions. Even when all the things pulling on you are good things, it creates tension and frustration. But if you add meaningful focus, you will live a profoundly meaningful life filled with *passionate equilibrium*—the exciting combination of passion expressed while maintaining your equilibrium or balance.

NO "SMOKE AND MIRRORS"

When we try something new, most of us want concrete proof that it will work—no smoke, no mirrors, no spin, just a simple demonstration that it really works. I have gathered substantial evidence that undertaking an intentional 2% Project—the action that gets you to your 2% Solution—is a transformational experience. My own 2% Solution began as an effort to align my work and my values. This soon evolved into a passion for helping others achieve an integrated engagement with life through their own 2% Solutions. For the past five years I have been interviewing professionals of all ages and from many walks of life about their 2% Projects. These stories are ones of joy and relief, of pain and transformation, and of learning to live in the flow. I have included some in this book to provide wisdom, humor, and inspiration as you embark on the path toward creating your own 2% Solution.

In 1993, my husband and I created our firm, Collaborative Growth, as a way of extending our support to those willing to step forward and achieve inspirational growth. In my research, I have found many people who have engaged in a variety of life-changing projects. What was the common thread? All of these people devoted at least 2% of their time for several months toward a project that has had a profound impact on their lives. Some of them started their 2% Projects in their workplaces when their organizations began making a concerted effort to engage their employees more fully. Others took it upon themselves to initiate their project to bring their *Esprit d'Core*—their true selves—alive after deciding that they were no longer satisfied in unfulfilling lives.

LIFE'S 2% SOLUTION: INSIDE THIS BOOK

You can choose to make an important difference in your life by implementing a 2% Project on your own. The guidance and exercises in this book are structured to help you succeed. It is not necessary that you join a group, hire a coach, or take any other formalized action. Many people work through this type of project and make the adjustments in their lives by themselves, as it is an intimate and very personal experience. Others choose to work in groups or to work with a coach. This is a choice you should make based on your personal needs, your learning style, and your circumstances. Regardless of whether you go after your 2% Solution alone, with a friend, a coach, or in a group, success comes from rolling up your sleeves and diving into your commitment. This is all about the quality of what you put into it, not about the quantity of time you give. Remember, you only need 2% of your time!

Within these pages you will find all you need to guide you in realizing your *Life's 2% Solution*, including these features and benefits:

- **Defining Moments**, which highlight key concepts and definitions

- **2% in Motion** profiles, which feature true stories of how to implement a 2% Project to achieve *Life's 2% Solution*

- **Activities and questionnaires** to help you identify your strengths and weaknesses and give you a personal inventory of the road ahead

- **Inspirational quotes** to buoy you along the way

- Discovery of your **Esprit d'Core**, or your spirit at the core of your being

- A **10-Step Action Plan** designed to help you reach your goal

In addition, you will engage in skill development to support your 2% Solution. Emotional and social intelligence, or EQ (for Emotional Quotient), is at the top of my list of most-needed skills. *Emotional intelligence* is based on ways of being intelligent that differ from the cognitive factors we typically measure with IQ. Whereas IQ involves analytical abilities and reasoning skills, EQ includes self-regard, empathy, and optimism—essential skills for building a happy life. For this reason, each chapter contains an **Engage Your EQ** skill-building activity, which draws on the work of experts such as Reuven Bar-On and Daniel Goleman.

Because of the wealth of material their systems offer on how to better understand ourselves and our world, we will be tapping into the work of some of the most forward-thinking people of our time. In particular, Don Beck's work on Spiral Dynamics integral, Ken Wilber's integral worldview, and the spiritual practices of those such as Father Thomas Keating have been very influential in my work. I recommend you consider them as well in your 2% journey.

In addition, you will find examples to help you identify and expand your strengths, for we know that successful application of our intelligence comes about only when we rely on our strengths. It is indisputable that enhancing our natural strengths is the strategy to bring our gifts to light. This is how we know we're *in the flow*, or as some people say, "in the zone."

You will find activities to assist you in growing the skills we discuss. I recommend you create a 2% Journal and record your responses there.

⌒

Success through a 2% Solution is usually a long and winding road, but it's well worth it. There are four fabulous, life-changing benefits that come from implementing your solution:

1. ***Zest Appeal.*** When you live from the zest of Esprit d'Core, you give your life the fullness and happiness that spontaneously flows from being committed to giving a voice to your inner wisdom.

2. ***Congruency.*** When you align your values with your daily living, there is true internal accountability, which creates authentic living that arises out of deep and honest personal reflection. It doesn't have to take a lot of time, but it does have to be honest.

3. ***Identity.*** When your identity is centered on your internal truth, you don't lose your bearings as normal lifecycle losses come your way. By learning to cope when you lose your outer labels, you know who you really are, without a photo ID.

4. ***Passionate Equilibrium.*** When you feel your passion for life renewing your world with balance and grace, you know you're living with passionate equilibrium.

In *Life's 2% Solution*, you'll meet real people living complicated lives like your own. They have used the 2% Solution to do things they thought were impossible. Some have fallen in love when they thought they were hopelessly single, while others quit decent jobs and hit pay dirt. Some traded in hefty heartaches tied to jumbo compensation packages for the simple life, while others healed long-standing, festering wounds from childhood, left addiction for sobriety, or grew in their spirituality. Their stories are inspiring; their results are transformational. I am honored to know each one of them.

Each of us seeks to live purposeful and happy lives. Once we meet our basic survival needs, we are universally called to a higher destiny that unfolds for us if we use our strengths to live authentically, aligned with a unique personal calling that fulfills our heart's desire. This is the essence of our humanity and is at the very core of a strong 2% Solution.

The 2% path takes courage—no doubt about it—yet the payoff is tremendous. The freedom you will gain from successfully completing your 2% Solution could range from the marvelous to the miraculous. Developing yourself through your 2% Solution gives you the opportunity to transform your life and live with passionate equilibrium. Some part of you knows this truth or you wouldn't be reading this book right now. Go for it—and enjoy your adventure in great living!

— Marcia Hughes
October 2005

1/

YOUR ESPRIT D'CORE
Connecting with Your Core Wisdom

Pulling open the large glass door, I smiled to myself as I stepped across the threshold into the impressive law office. I was about to begin my high-flying career as a legal eagle. The thrill was short-lived, however. Almost immediately I began to experience tension that had nothing to do with the stress of long hours. The structure and values of the traditional law firm where I worked distressed me deeply. It seemed that at the office I was required to be someone different from who I was in the rest of my life. It left me off-balance and disconnected. I was having such an enormous crisis of identity that I abruptly took three weeks off and went on a Vision Quest in Death Valley.

With no distractions and nothing to do but think and feel, I sat on a desolate crag of brown volcanic rock and pondered the huge disconnect I was feeling in my career. Of all the expectations I had had about being a lawyer, this was certainly not among them; I felt completely ambushed.

Gradually, my defenses, along with the neatly compartmentalized aspects of myself, began to fall away and allow my core being—the true me—to surface. With the endless blue sky and cacti as my witnesses, I made a promise to myself that I would integrate my personal and professional lives. Yet I was immediately confronted with the enormity of this seemingly impossible task—the ramifications of this promise to myself were daunting. Little did I know that that moment was the inauspicious beginning of the first-ever 2% Solution! Nor did I have any idea how profoundly it would change my life.

That was in 1981. In some way, every day since that day, I've focused on how to bring together this fundamental connection between meaning and action for myself and others. I have discovered that not only is it possible to integrate my professional and spiritual selves, for me it is essential. It is fundamental to the essence of who I am—my Esprit d'Core. %

Discovering, claiming, and integrating your own individual Esprit d'Core is the lynchpin to becoming a fulfilled, happy, and effective person. Once a person recognizes and awakens his or her own Esprit d'Core—in other words, gets his or her calling—it usually ignites a fiery quest, propelling a person on a journey to his or her signature 2% Solution.

Remember Bruce Wayne had his red Batphone? Sure, superheroes may have more gizmos and contraptions that make the call seem more dramatic, but we all get a call, one way or another. Sometimes it feels like someone is pounding on the door; other times it feels like a barely audible whisper. Yet, the call comes through.

For me, the call and the question I faced was, "*How can I bring my gifts to light fully and honestly in my personal, professional, and spiritual lives?*" The path wasn't at all clear. It was a discovery process to learn that there are so many ways to be of true and valuable service. Acting in a way that connects meaning and action is the realization of your own Esprit d'Core.

YOUR CORE IS CALLING

Esprit d'Core is that which brings life to you at your core innermost self—it's the combination that when turned, aligns the tumblers and opens the vault within your heart containing the treasure you are meant to bring into the world. The purpose of this book is to offer a path inward to help you discover and affirm your Esprit d'Core, and then set it loose. It is very much like your own genie waiting for you to open the bottle and let it out. Once you bring out your Esprit d'Core, you can start making your dreams and wishes come true.

A DEFINING MOMENT

Esprit d'Core is the spirit at the core of our being. It is that unique element that makes up one's fundamental core self. It dwells in our innermost self. Our core spirit must be integrated and expressed in our daily living in order to be fulfilled and happy.

When I created the concept of Esprit d'Core, I was inspired by the term *esprit de corps*, which is defined as "the selfless and often enthusiastic and jealous devotion of the members of a group or association of persons to the group or to its purposes." In both phrases, the heart of the meaning is based on the word *esprit*, which, according to *The Oxford English Dictionary*, was first used by a Frenchman in 1591, and means "spirit mind," or cleverness and vivacity. *Esprit* is also linked to the Latin word for spirit, defined as "the breath of life." It is inseparable from our breath, and thus one cannot be alive without a spirit connection. If you aren't connected to your Esprit d'Core, your body is alive while your spirit is locked, deadening you to a meaningful engagement with life.

> An association must have esprit de corps which induces its members to put the welfare of the institution above their own.
>
> —Peter Drucker

Esprit d'Core refers to the spirit at the core of your being. It's that which you would claim if you had the opportunity to choose one passion to express without regard to anything else. It's your personal calling, and it awaits you. You know you are living from your Esprit d'Core when your smile is bigger, you aren't questioning yourself, and you relax into your real self. Paradoxically, you might feel bigger *and* smaller—bigger because you aren't so constricted (all of you is alive) and smaller because it's not such a struggle.

Discovering your Esprit d'Core is the first essential step in achieving your personal 2% Solution. This is closely followed by designing and implementing your own 2% Project, because the 2% Solution is all about finding the calling in your heart and giving it a voice. It's taking 2% of your time to respond to what's knocking on your inner door—to find who's calling on your Batphone. It's finding the joy in the flow of life.

> **A DEFINING MOMENT**
>
> A **2% Project** is the *method* for achieving your 2% Solution. If you've got a great sense of direction, think of it as a road map. If you're a manager, you might think of it as a business plan. If you're a chef, it's the recipe. If you're an artist, it's the paint, the musical score, the dance steps.

What's remarkable and truly exciting is that experiencing the joy of living in the flow of life is possible because it only requires 2% of our time. It's not about giving up our whole life as we know it, but nurturing our life and expanding its depth. It's about allowing ourselves to be and to act inspired. We bring the 2% Solution to our lives by implementing a 2% Project that resonates with our own Esprit d'Core. Live to express your gift by giving your heart's calling 2% of your time every day, not just those rare stolen days.

Your 2% Project is your daily focus. You'll spend 30 minutes a day for 6 months or even years implementing your 2% Project by following the 10 steps described in Chapter 2. A sample action plan and plenty of tips will guide you in starting and following through on this promising journey.

THE DAILY GRIND

I owe, I owe, so off to work I go.
No pain, no gain.

The attitudes reflected by these popular bumper stickers demonstrate a common sentiment found among business professionals today. Most professionals spend more time at work than in any other part of their lives—yet if this is the attitude we have about our work, how much joy and fulfillment can we expect to find there? Not much! This pain is often manifested by chronic job dissatisfaction that has its roots in workplaces that lack vision, have no heart, and lack cohesive strategy. Trading pain for joy happens when meaning and action are connected, when intention and purpose drive activities and choices.

Implementing a 2% Project as an individual or as a work team is a way to connect those dots. It's a way to live for our "days on," not our "days off." This book demonstrates a simple process for transforming your life to a series of "days on." Ultimately, this is a unique strategy of living with passion and balance that I call *passionate equilibrium*. Passionate equilibrium is the ultimate high. It beats a day at the spa, a World Series-winning home run, a romantic getaway, a trip to your favorite vacation destination . . .but we'll get to all that in Chapter 5.

RETURNING TO CREATIVITY

Many people report feeling constrained by the seemingly inflexible and staid environments in which they work. The organizational structure is often hierarchical and the corporate culture frequently promotes learned powerlessness. I regularly hear a painful refrain by professionals who struggle with compromised working conditions and wonder how to unleash creativity. It's the pain well articulated in this extract from an anonymous poem:

> *The song I came to sing is left*
> *Unsung, I spent my life stringing and*
> *Unstringing my instrument.*

I can't count all the people whom I have heard cry with the pain so well articulated by this lament. Is this cry yours as well? If so, it *can* change! You can embrace a 2% Solution for yourself.

2% in Motion

WASH, RINSE, REPEAT

At age 40, Carlos decided to do an inventory. His life wasn't bad; it just didn't have the spark he suspected should be there. Carlos felt he could hear his song in the distance, but he surely wasn't singing it out loud and strong.

But he didn't know how to make the change—or even what to change. So he listed and relisted the issues and problems that troubled him. He hunted for the common threads. He found some, tested, and then tried again. Carlos sums it up in the words he always heard from his practical mother, "Wash, rinse, repeat!" Finally he hit on his 2% Project, which he phrases as "focusing on expressing my spirit." He realized his low assertiveness meant his voice was often buried. Carlos knew he wanted a real change, so he diligently worked with this exciting concept to gain a concrete handle on what to do. He wanted specifics to make it operational.

Carlos decided to pay careful attention to how well he expressed his own opinions. At the end of each day he would take 15 to 30 minutes to reflect on the day, noting when he had spoken up and when he had stayed too quiet. He also asked two trusted colleagues to have coffee with him a few times a week every week for several months so he could regularly receive their insightful feedback. At first, Carlos was dismayed to recognize that his song was so quiet that his impact at work and on the rest of his life was greatly minimalized. Where was his voice, anyway? Carlos realized how quiet and unassuming he had been.

He noticed, received feedback, wrote, and thought it over. He made a personal promise not to beat himself up when he recognized times he should have spoken up but didn't. Rather, he would notice and commit to correct the behavior at the next opportunity. This kept him resilient and happy to be in the change mode.

Carlos reports positive results: he discovered why many decisions in his life had lacked a foundation, and he learned to decide more issues for himself. He is finding the difference to be a subtle one. He comments that while his day-to-day existence isn't remarkably different externally, he feels much more at ease and more effective. He *looks pleased as he reports that he is more attuned to his desires and the motivations of his coworkers, thus making him a more effective manager. He is enjoying exploring new thoughts and ideas. Carlos's conclusion: "My personal opinions about my life and self hold more weight in the world than I had imagined."* %

Imagine what would happen if more professionals could pour their creativity into their work. Indeed, there is a long legacy of organizations stifling creativity. The prevalent orientation to a mechanistic approach to life was heavily influenced by the Age of Enlightenment, which occurred in the 18th century. At that time rationalism began to drive society in a precise and engineered manner. While the approach yielded tremendous technical developments, it also gave way to specialization.

That approach is now widely recognized as being the source of alienation for employees from their true talents, since narrow specialization prevents employees from unleashing their full creativity. Studies indicate that alienation and disengagement come with significant costs. The more emotionally engaged an employee is, the more productive the employee, and the more profitable the company. Curt Coffman and Gabriel Gonzalez-Molina, authors of *Follow This Path* (2002) and management consultants for the Gallup Organization, provide statistical analyses of extensive survey data to prove that companies profit when workers and customers feel appreciated and listened to.

> Our mind, once stretched by a new idea, never regains its original dimensions.
>
> —Oliver Wendell Holmes, Jr.

Many of us spend more time at work or on our careers than in any other part of our lives. The stifled feeling so many employees report is a clear indication that most people need more room to be able to express themselves more fully and honestly. To be fully motivated, we must have room for our spirit to soar so we can feel we're giving expression to our Esprit d'Core.

Ironically, I often find it is actually the professionals who already have started a path of inquiry—who are doing soul-searching—who are encountering the greatest pain. It might be because they are coming out of the numbness that captures so many of us. Pain can be a motivator—a gift to give us that extra "pinch to grow an inch." These folks have begun asking questions, recognizing that more is possible, and the buds of hope are beginning to blossom. They may be asking more of their workplace than ever—beginning to insist on new ways of connecting the dots of meaning and action. This effort is rewarded at times, but it is often discouraged, even if only because of lack of understanding. Imagine the frozen possibilities. Yet knowing that there are bumps in the road and doors that remain closed *isn't* reason not to engage in this transformative process; it *is* reason to act with patience as well as diligence.

Early management practitioners believed that financial rewards would provide the incentive for workers to become more productive. However, a plethora of research shows otherwise. Gallup has found that the number one workplace concern of employees is how their first-level manager treats them. Any manager who encourages the "whole employee," who encourages creativity, will have a much more resilient workforce and one with lower turnover. Interestingly, it's this process of giving up the exclusive focus on the dollar that creates the environment for profit to grow.

Something different is needed. Workers are noticeably less satisfied in the world of "do more with less," reduced loyalty from organizations to employees, and the increasing frantic pace with expectations to produce good results often without sufficient resources. This crushing scenario is a call for action. The 2% Solution offers a path for individuals to give a little bit of time to provide their heart's desire some airtime, which will consequently greatly increase the engagement with their profession, their job, and their life. Whether you're interested in the 2% Solution for yourself at home, at work, or to support those you work with, it offers great promise for bringing full value to your venture.

SIGNS THAT YOU'RE LOST IN SPACE

Sometimes it feels like you're floating in the darkness, your feet no longer planted on terra firma. Is your life proceeding on autopilot? You may be in need of a 2% Solution. Honest self-reflection can help you assess whether you are in a free fall. Take a look at the questions in the following activity and see how you respond.

Activity: *Taking My Pulse*

1. Am I busy, busy, busy, but not feeling like I'm getting anywhere, or accomplishing anything meaningful?

    ○ Yes (A)
    ○ I'm partially satisfied, but still feeling antsy (B)
    ○ No (C)

2. When someone brings me an interesting new possibility, do I find myself saying, "Yes, this is important/exciting, but I'm busy now, I'll get back soon?" However, I know I probably won't.

    ○ Very often (A)
    ○ Sometimes (B)
    ○ Almost never (C)

(I refer to this as the "busy back soon" principle, so well articulated in *The Tao of Pooh* by Benjamin Hoff. Yet how often do you actually get back to the person or the opportunity? How often do you just rush forward? How dissatisfying is this response pattern?)

3. How often do I find myself getting snippy, grouchy, doing lackluster work, though I truly want to do better? Can I see the possibility of a meaningful engagement, but just can't get there?

    This happens:
    ○ Frequently (A)
    ○ Sometimes (B)
    ○ Rarely (C)

4. Am I worried that when my life ends I won't have "sung my song?" As the poem laments, will I have

"strung and unstrung my instrument" over and over and over?

    ○ This is a big worry (A)
    ○ It's not a big worry, but it does gnaw at me (B)
    ○ This is not a concern (C)

5. Do I recognize a yearning to bring another part of me alive? Do I hold back because of a fear that it'll turn my life upside down, and that's just too risky so I don't venture any action?

    I have this yearning
    ○ A lot (A)
    ○ Some (B)
    ○ Not much (C)

6. Do I regularly experience any of these? (Write in an A if you feel it a lot, a B if it's sometimes, and a C if it's not an issue.)

    ___ Feeling trapped.
    ___ I keep saying to myself, "I once had so much hope for what I'd do. Now it's not much."
    ___ A deep yearning to be more creative.
    ___ Fantasies about "running away from home" and leaving my current life behind.
    ___ Depression.
    ___ Anger that spills out at the most surprising times.

Now, pause. Take some time to reflect on your answers. What are you noticing? Do your responses lead you to a nagging feeling that you'd like to be more fulfilled, more whole, but you just don't know how to get there? Or perhaps you think it's impossible given how overcommitted you already are. There's hope! Keep reading.

Calculate your score. Give yourself 10 points for every A, 5 for every B, and 0 for every C. Then add up all your points. If your response is:

0–25 You are feeling well engaged with life. Check to see if you already have something similar to the 2% Solution in place in your life. If so, this book can help you fine-tune it and go for the gold. If you don't have a 2% Solution, consider starting one to take your life to an even more exciting level.

30–55 Your life probably has many satisfying aspects, but there are some troubling elements that a 2% Solution could help you address to make you feel freer and more alive.

60–110 Get started on your 2% Solution now! It will help provide the alignment you long for.

If these factors are kicking you in the seat of your pants, take stock *now*! Seriously consider starting your 2% Solution—or if you've got one going, sharpen the focus. The 2% Solution entails finding the deep calling in your heart and giving it a voice. Remember, you only need to find 2% of your time—that's about 30 minutes a day—to change your life. It's all about quality, not quantity. If you have a short attention span, this is for you! If you get interrupted all the time, this has your name all over it!

Hope is the thing with feathers
That perches in the soul,
And sings the tune without the words,
And never stops at all

—Emily Dickinson, Collected Poems

You will find testaments   throughout this book from professionals who have implemented 2% Solutions and found that it actually causes all of life to work better. As Stephen Covey writes in *The 7 Habits of Highly Effective People*, if you use this to "sharpen the saw," then everything else is more fine-tuned and functional.

2% in Motion

ODE TO JOY

Joy has worked through many permutations of her evolving career. She's moved from public speaking and training to online training to running her own flower shop; now she's working full time in organizational development for an engineering firm. Through these diverse career moves, Joy has experienced peaks and valleys, highs and lows. A naturally happy person, she has spent much of her great talent and energy on exceeding the expectations of others rather than meeting her own needs.

At first Joy was mildly annoyed by her own accommodating behavior, until it finally captured all her attention and she had to make changes. Opening her own flower shop was part of her response. But this didn't happen lightly; she'd spent years in deep inquiry. Joy is a classic example of today's employee who has capitalized on the organizational training she has received and blended that with her own seeking to be the full expression of herself. Her 2% Project was to better understand what she wanted for herself and to stand up for her right to accomplish those goals. Her life's 2% Solution is learning to assert herself while knowing that she's always engaged in the journey. She's learning to recognize both the predictable and the surprising components.

Joy is successful in her multiple endeavors because she has developed a four-star strategy, which reflects the four central themes supporting the 2% Process:

1. ***She uses the full palette.*** *Personalities and thinking styles are often described with colors, and Joy uses all of them as needed, integrating various styles in her work. I refer to this as "whole-mind integration." (This is Strategy #1: Operating with an integrated, whole-mind approach.)*

2. ***She operates from abundance.*** *Joy knows her own strengths and recognizes that they are resources to fuel success. She capitalizes on her strengths and*

gets the most out of them while minimizing her weaknesses. (Strategy #2: Focusing on enhancing your strengths.)

3. **She "walks her talk."** Joy's values drive her choices, and she respects the values others hold, though they may differ from hers. (Strategy #3: Understanding and applying your values and respecting those of others.)

4. **She has heart smarts.** Joy knows that success depends more on using her emotional intelligence (EQ) than her IQ. (Strategy #4: Integrating all the strategies into learning as you grow your emotional intelligence.)

Each of these four strategies is central to achieving your own 2% Solution. The three skills of operating within your strengths, your values, and using a whole-mind approach all come together to enhance your emotional intelligence. Hence we will work throughout this book on how to develop each of these skills.

Joy expanded her whole-mind integration by understanding her thinking and behaving preferences. She found that she most prefers to think using the right side of her brain—to make people connections and by being conceptual. However, she also thrives on using her analytical skills to understand the data behind any endeavor she's planning. For a job to work for Joy, she needs to have outlets for all of her thinking preferences. Owning her own business allowed her to use all those preferences while expanding her emotional intelligence, especially her self-awareness and empathy.

Then she did some reality testing and discovered that she'd been working too hard to make a profit. Now she's using her greatly expanded awareness in her new salaried position in organizational development for an engineering company and has time for a lot of fun. Her last e-mail reported that she and her husband were off on a Montana motorcycle tour followed by the Albuquerque balloon *festival. Her hard work and deep attention to her 2% Solution led Joy to write me, "Yes! Life is great!" Her 2% Solution is teaching her that life is a journey, not a destination.* %

BEING IN THE FLOW

When I was in college and later when practicing law, you'd find me on the Colorado slopes skiing at least one day a week in the winter. Getting up on the top of the mountain, seeing the incredible vistas, and then using all my concentration to navigate the tall moguls completely captured my attention. I simply couldn't worry about classes or clients. I loved my time on the mountain—it was absolutely refreshing to get completely away from school and later from my work and not to have any worries. At this stage in my life, I've turned to salsa dancing for a break from it all. I can't possibly glide one step forward, two backward, while worrying about a meeting, a project, or a seminar—my soul simply loves the break!

These kinds of experiences typify what it's like to be in the flow.

Flow can be experienced in these small parts of our lives or brought to our whole life. The 2% Solution can make it happen by giving you a structured and creative way to bring about a meaningful integration of your heart's calling into your life. This state at its finest is demonstrated by real-life figures such as the Dalai Lama, athletes like bicyclist Lance Armstrong, and even mythic figures such as Luke Skywalker. You don't need to be a superstar or a science fiction superhero to be in a state of flow—anyone can do it!

Esprit d'Core comes from the resonate joy that springs forth when we are truly "in the flow," as Mihaly Csikszentmihalyi, author of *Flow* (1990), would say. According to Csikszentmihalyi, the optimal experience is based on the concept of flow—"the state in which people are so involved in an activity that nothing else seems to matter; the experience itself is so enjoyable that people will do it even at great cost, for the sheer sake of doing it"(4). He states that the key component of an optimal experience is that it is an end in itself. The activity becomes intrinsically rewarding—*autotelic.*

A DEFINING MOMENT

Mihaly Csikszentmihalyi defines an **autotelic** activity as a "self-contained activity, one that is done not with the expectation of some future benefit, but simply because the doing itself is the reward."

Csikszentmihalyi's research provides an important clarification of the 2% Process. He contrasts autotelic with exotelic activities. Autotelic activities are done for the sheer joy of the experience, while *exotelic* ones are done for external reasons. It's the difference between going for a walk because exercising is the responsible thing to do or going for a walk to enjoy movement and the surrounding beauty.

It is likely that when we begin a 2% Project it will be largely exotelic, or done for external reasons. That is, we'll start it because the concept is convincing enough to give it a chance, and we suspect it'll make a functional difference in our life. With sufficient engagement in the process, it is likely to convert to an intrinsically rewarding activity—though, of course, few things are completely one or the other. You may encounter challenges as the process becomes more autotelic. These challenges frequently unfold as personal moments of truth that can no longer be avoided, and they are a natural part of a long-term 2% Solution.

You are likely to have times of flow and times of challenge. New growth cycles often contain some chaffing, some resistance, until a new level of competence is reached. Those who have had a 2% Project under-way for several years report that "it hasn't always been easy." The universal report, though, by 2% practitioners is that when they were willing to hang in through the difficult times, the growth was exponential. My 2% Project has grown from the recognition on that Vision Quest in Death Valley I mentioned at the beginning of this chapter through countless sagas and stages. I've journaled, participated in leadership groups, meditated, and hiked as I've continued dancing with the question of how to integrate my professional and spiritual callings. Each step has helped me live more honestly. Though it's been difficult at times, the rewards from sticking with it are profound.

Implementing a 2% Project is a way to learn how to live "in the zone." This is significant, as many desire to experience flow yet are frustrated by how amorphous, how unobtainable this state seems to be. We've all heard about examples of living in the flow such as

Olympians experience. (And it's just as true for those in the Special Olympics, such as my daughter Julia. When she's swimming in competition, she's fully engaged, she receives immediate feedback, and she loves it!)

LIFE ON THE FAST TRACK

It's not just your perception that things are speeding up. It's reality. In *Waking Up in Time* (1998, *xi*), Peter Russell, a student of Stephen Hawking and a big-picture thinker with degrees in theoretical physics, psychology, and computer science, validates our perceptions that everything is speeding up.

> *Why does evolution accelerate? The answer lies in the fact that new evolutionary breakthroughs often facilitate future advances. Multicellular organisms, sexual reproduction, and the emergence of nervous systems have all done their part to hasten the pace of evolutionary change. Now, with the emergence of human beings, two new features are speeding development yet further. Speech allows us to share our experiences and understandings with each other, giving us the ability to accumulate a collective body of knowledge. Our hands, which are among the most versatile organs Nature has evolved, have given us the ability to take the clay of Mother Earth and reshape it to our own ends. Combining these two evolutionary breakthroughs has made us the most creative species this planet has ever known. And the more we apply that creativity, the faster things change.*

We know that creativity in the workplace is essential to keeping employees happy and also dramatically affects the bottom line, yet Peter Russell is pointing out the creativity conundrum—the more creative we are, the faster life moves and the harder we struggle with the pace!

The million-dollar questions are: "How do we reap the benefits of this rapid-fire momentum and keep our sanity? How do we experience peace in the midst of the turmoil of change? How do we use this to facilitate our own momentum?"

First, we benefit by more fully taking stock of how this evolutionary pace is affecting us. Childre and Martin, authors of *The Heartmath Solution*, present powerful information on the heart, including the distinct brain around the heart and how it influences our thinking and behaving choices. We will consider this approach more in Chapter 8 when we review the benefits and strategies for exercising whole-mind thinking; for now, let's look at the evidence they present on stress and its consequences to us. The authors state:

> The challenge we face is to achieve greater levels of internal coherence in an age of increasing chaos, complexity, and incoherence. It's no longer enough to be smart. We need a new kind of intelligence that's quicker, more reliable, and more flexible than the linear, step-by-step intelligence we're accustomed to using. (51)

Thus chaos, complexity, and incoherence lead to great stress. Their research shows that one of the greatest causes is the tremendous speed with which we have to shift concepts or focus on too many different tasks many times an hour. They found that "it's not unusual for a person to deal with ten or twenty (or even more) concept shifts in an hour (topping one hundred shifts in a single eight- to ten-hour workday)" (51). Their strategy is to increase internal coherence by linking the heart with the head. It's a compelling strategy and one we'll work with in subsequent chapters.

Additionally, saying yes to the momentum, rather than trying to fight it, is another strategy for success. This builds on Thomas Crum's creative work about conflict. In *The Magic of Conflict,* Crum brings us to an unavoidable truth. Conflict is neither good nor bad; it just is. I've used his work in my mediation and conflict resolution work for years in my company, Collaborative Growth, and audiences quickly grasp the power of his message. The question is how resourceful our response will be when we feel challenged. We can make conflict a gift in our lives. Similarly, we can say yes to the evolutionary momentum and allow it to lead us to greater potential. The choice is ours—and the impact of the choice is dramatic.

Yes, the pace of evolution is dramatically influencing our sense of peace and productivity, truly everything. It takes a conscious process of engagement with the world to work well with this ever-changing dynamic. That process is the 2% Solution.

Engage Your EQ

Emotions are contagious—"smile and the world smiles with you." Daniel Goleman and his co-authors of *Primal Leadership* describe numerous studies documenting this principle. They cite a Yale University School of Management study that found that we are affected by other's emotions (10). The study by Sigal Barsade and Donald Gibson, found positive emotions have the most influence generally in this order:

1. Laughter
2. Cheerfulness and warmth
3. Irritability
4. Depression

Fortunately, evolution has benefited from this order of contagion!

Similarly, as we just considered, there is evolutionary momentum demanding that we truly do our best to satisfy our sense of our "calling," our life's purpose. That deep yearning in your heart—the one that just won't let you go—has evolutionary purpose, which is directly connected with your exercise of your emotional intelligence.

Extrapolating from the definition of emotional and social intelligence by Bar-On, I work with this definition: **Emotional and social intelligence** is a concept that reflects our ability to understand, express, and manage our emotions as well as those of others. It also includes the ability to cope with life's pressures in order to realize success.

Emotional intelligence, EI, and EQ are equivalent terms. The good news is that while IQ is considered relatively fixed at birth, you can grow your EQ. That's important because research shows that EQ contributes to 27% to 45% or more of workplace success, while IQ contributes 1% to 20% (Stein and Book, 2000, 17). The 2% Solution is a key tool for enhancing your EQ; you'll learn how by working with the descriptions and developmental ideas in this book.

Bar-On's Emotional Quotient Inventory® (EQi) is a personal skills measure that is sold worldwide. As one of the best and most popular interpretations of emotional intelligence, I find it an excellent guide to understanding how to interpret and grow your emotional intelligence. Because the EQi is based on social as well as emotional skills, the 15 competencies addressed are an excellent tool for learning how to live authentically. The 15 EQi skills are clustered in 5 component areas, as discussed by Marilyn Gowing in her comparison of primary EQ measures (2001, 108). They are:

Intrapersonal
Self-Regard
Emotional Self-Awareness
Independence
Assertiveness
Self-Actualization

Interpersonal
Interpersonal Relationships
Empathy
Social Responsibility

Adaptability
Reality Testing
Flexibility
Problem Solving

Stress Management
Stress Tolerance
Impulse Control

General Mood
Optimism
Happiness

SELF-ACTUALIZATION: THE ULTIMATE GOAL

The call to become all that we can be is one of our greatest gifts. The term often used to describe this motivational reach is *self-actualization*. If the term evokes images of gurus or monks, prepare to be surprised. In their book *The EQ Edge*, Stein and Book discuss the top five factors of emotional intelligence that contribute to professionals being successful.

The first of the five is self-actualization! (For those of you who can't bear not knowing the other four factors, they are happiness, optimism, self-regard, and assertiveness. We'll discuss how to grow each of these factors in the following chapters.)

A DEFINING MOMENT

Bar-On defines **self-actualization** as it is used in the EQi as "the process of striving to actualize one's potential capacity, abilities, and talents. It requires the ability and drive to set and achieve goals. It is characterized by being involved in and feeling committed to various interests and pursuits. Self-actualization is a life-long effort leading to the enrichment of life" (Bar-On, 2001, 89).

The 2% Solution is a direct path to unfolding self-actualization in your life. It is a key to finding and aligning motivation, and that translates to effectiveness. This is a critical skill that successful professionals routinely demonstrate. These are individuals who meet their potential throughout their lives in the workplace, in the community, and in their homes.

In Chapter 5 and throughout the book, we will explore the fourth benefit of the 2% Solution—passionate equilibrium—which is directly linked to expanding self-actualization. The first step in growing this EI skill is to notice and direct your motivation. The quiz in the following activity will get you started.

Activity: *Your Motivation Quotient*

1. On a scale of 1 to 10, with 10 being the highest, how motivated are you to meet your top goals?

2. Why?

3. What motivates you?

4. How do you know?

5. If you're bored, is it because you're afraid to make a commitment to something important to you?

6. If you are afraid—or just might be, you're not sure—what might be the fear?

7. Is it worth stifling your motivations?

8. In the game of life, are you hitting par or are you buried in the rough far from the green? Do you want to do anything to upgrade your answer? If so, what?

These questions are just for you, so love yourself enough to be honest!

Only you can define what self-actualization is for you. However, the link between this aligned motivation, your social and emotional intelligence, and your success is unequivocal.

TUNE IN YOUR MIND

- Listen to the calling in your heart; it is that unique thing you long to do. There is a specific path you can follow to give it a voice and begin living authentically.

- Learn through 2% in Motion—these are the stories of others who have gained so much from the 2% Process. They are full of teachable moments.

- Embrace the evolutionary momentum which can become the trajectory for getting your life on track.

- Notice what motivates you. Are you developing your emotional intelligence skill of self-actualization?

TUNE OUT THE NOISE

- Avoid the trap of thinking you can only have a meaningful life if you change everything.

- If you can't name times when you are in the flow, then make it a priority. Find out how to live in sync!

A SNEAK PREVIEW

Chapter 2 will highlight more of what the 2% Solution offers you. It will provide the tools to help you define your own 2% Project and begin your 10-Step Action Plan. Claim time for yourself by focusing on your EI skill of assertiveness as you initiate your 2% Project.

2/

MAKING IT YOURS
Creating a 10-Step Action Plan

Bonnie was a passionate, enthusiastic, and successful executive with a reputation for no-holds-barred truth-telling and getting the job done. But she didn't tell anyone her most personal truth: a feeling of emptiness dogged her. Finally frustrated enough by her loneliness to commit to action, she embarked upon a 2% Project to get to the bottom of the hole in her soul. With the help of a gifted therapist, Bonnie discovered the personal barriers she'd erected that prevented an intimate relationship. She was emotionally cautious with men she dated—careful to not have or talk about many feelings.

Once she realized this, Bonnie began to apply her notorious truth-telling and results-oriented approach to this very painful issue. Soon, she kicked into high gear. Her 2% Project was a particularly tough one, because it didn't have a tidy goal, such as a career shift. While a career change isn't easy, it is well-defined, making the action plan simpler to identify, whereas a fundamental shift in one's personal life is all the more amorphous.

Bonnie defined her 2% Project as truth-telling and truthful living even when she felt vulnerable. She had no idea where such a quest would lead, but she knew she had to stop kidding herself if she want- ed to heal the emptiness she felt. It was a tremendous leap of faith. She was in for a few surprises! Because of the benefits of her 2%

Project, Bonnie ultimately welcomed a partner into her life, moved to a new city, and found a challenging new job. Through her ongoing 2% work, and years after her therapy was completed, she continues to employ scrupulous honesty in opening up to relationships with genuine depth. %

Defining and implementing a 2% Solution is a journey. A select few of us know immediately what we are called to do; for most of us, however, the definition unfolds over time—and may change along the way. Additionally, implementing your 2% Solution is a living, dynamic process, and it generally proceeds in 10 steps. While there is a likely order, you will find changes occur in response to what's happening in your life. A step may repeat or naturally occur early for you. Some steps may repeat themselves as your learning deepens. It is more important for you to find your flow than to be concerned with the order. Some people prefer to get the whole story (i.e., reading this book from cover to cover) and then start the process, while others like to dive in and be personally engaged while learning about it. We all learn and respond to things based on our own preferred styles, so choose the way that works best for you.

As discussed in Chapter 1, you may start out without any clear idea about what your own Esprit d'Core calls you to do and be, but it will become clear if you trust this plan. In this chapter you will:

- Learn the 10-Step Action Plan to implement your personal 2% Solution

- Sketch out the framework of your own 2% Project

- Decide how to integrate your deepest values into your 2% Project

- Explore the eight developmental value clusters and how they influence your motivation

- Enhance your EQ skill of assertiveness as you claim time for yourself and act on your 2% Project

When Bonnie began her 2% Solution, she was unaccustomed to opening up and sharing her feelings and concerns with close friends, especially with men she was dating. She didn't even know what her internal feelings were much of the time. Learning to tell the truth about how she felt meant that she had to remove the internal barriers to *knowing* how she felt. She also had to confront the feeling that it wasn't safe to discuss her feelings when she was developing a relationship with a man. This took courage! It will take courage for you to challenge your own barriers as well, and as your courage grows to support your vision, the results will carry you through—not only for your initial 2% Project, but for your lifelong 2% Solution.

Bonnie chose to be willing to know what she was feeling and why, and to share appropriately what she discovered with the people in her life, especially when she was developing an intimate relationship. Out of this Bonnie learned to open up to her life, and now she has a husband and a child—a far grander reward than she knew would come from spending 2% of her time to be more aware and honest with herself and others!

TAKING ON ONE MORE THING?

We are about to jump into action! Are you ready? It is understandable if you have mixed feelings. It's exciting to give a potentially profound gift to yourself, but you may be asking yourself, "How can I add one more thing to my life? Some days it's hard to find time to brush my teeth—where will I find 30 minutes?" Confusion, frustration, hope, and worry are all normal responses when we contemplate taking on something new, especially something with the potential to be truly transformative.

Recognize the positive intent behind your resistance. It may sound strange, but have a conversation with the resistance. Let yourself "be the resistance" and speak and write from that perspective. Learn what is really holding you back. If you are still hesitant, read through this chapter to understand the concept and gain perspective from the stories of others—then decide if you are ready to give yourself this gift. You will already be practicing a key part of the 2% Process, which is to engage in honest self-inquiry. Every step you take to enhance your conscious engagement with life will be progress. Caution: Don't get caught in paralysis by analysis. You could end up thinking *about* it for so long that you never act, and that would be a real loss.

Your conversation with yourself might sound something like this:

GO: Yes, I'm starting the project now. I don't want to keep on spending my time on things that don't fulfill me. I'm tired of being crabby, out of sorts, and feeling so stressed. I work too hard to feel like all the good stuff happens to other people. I deserve more, and this is a reasonable time commitment to invest in myself. I deserve it.

STOP: You're kidding, right? You struggle with all the to-dos that aren't done already. How can you consider adding something else? Besides, I'm tired.

GO: I know, I know. But I think this will help me get over the tiredness; it will give me something to look forward to, a reason to have more zest in my life. I spend more than 30 minutes a day on lots of other people and priorities. I need something for *me*. I need enhanced personal value and purpose.

STOP: Yes, but just make a list of "why nots" and I'll win; you can't find the time. I guarantee it.

GO: Now that's a challenge! I'll make of list of "whys" and "why nots" and sort it out. I need more balance in my life, that's for sure. Maybe it will give me a clearer picture about why I seem to do such much but enjoy it so little—lots of the time.

Activity: *Making a List and Checking It Twice*

Grab a pen, get a beverage, and get comfortable. Make a list here or in your 2% Journal of reasons for doing a 2% Project and for not doing one. Be honest! Use the following chart to help organize your thoughts. After you've made your list, go do something else for awhile, then come back later and review it. What did you discover? Is your resistance a stall tactic to avoid something? It is much better to address the resistance now rather than to let it fester.

For	Against	Comments

THE 10-STEP ACTION PLAN

Easier than the 10 Commandments, more reliable than the pop music charts, here are the 10 steps for executing your 2% Project. We will work with these steps throughout the book, so you may find it helpful to bookmark this page.

1. *Understand the process.* As you read through *Life's 2% Solution*, question whether you are ready to fully engage in the 2% Process. This commitment by itself will be transformative.

2. *Write down the goal of your 2% Solution and keep it readily accessible.* Knowing where you're headed is half the journey. Then begin to focus on your 2% Project, which will bring your long-term 2% Solution to life. It's important to focus on the details of your 2% Project. Where are you going? How will you get there? This is a part of experiencing "flow" as you implement your 2% Solution.

3. *Engage in a reflective process to refine your personal 2% Project.* Developing a reflective lifestyle and bringing more meaning to your life will support your becoming increasingly clear about your true identity. Consider buying a journal, labeling it your "2% Journal," and using it for the activities and your reflections as you go through this book. You may find your journal will be a best friend for years as you take 2% notes!

4. *Design a routine.* You need to find 2% of your time on a regular basis to work on your project. Structure it so that it works for your lifestyle. Maybe it is 30 minutes every day, or perhaps one larger block of time weekly suits you better. Get out your calendar and schedule it as you would any important appointment.

5. *Implement the first steps of your action plan to get your project underway.* Pay attention to how your project is serving you. You will add to it as you gain increasing perspective and a sense of how to structure your project into your life.

6. *Imagine your anticipated results.* Project out to the future and do a litmus test of your project with all your senses. If your project is successfully incorporated into your life, will it make the difference you are welcoming?

7. *Recalibrate.* You will need to retool occasionally to keep your project unfolding toward your goal. Be particularly vigilant when you come upon a difficult moment or a painful choice that calls for courage. These are moments when it's easier to just change than to roll up your sleeves and do the hard work. Readjust your action plan when needed, and find your inner strength when necessary.

8. *Seek feedback from meaningful people in your life.* Mentors and others you respect can help you decide whether your process is on target. You can get feedback in a variety of ways. Work with a supportive group where you reflect with one another on your process, use a coach, a therapist, or talk with someone you respect.

9. *Enjoy*! You are engaged in this endeavor as a gift to yourself to promote a life well lived. Happiness and optimism are significant aspects of emotional intelligence.

10. *Focus on singing your song, not on restringing your instrument.* Imagine your anticipated results. Continue the process you began in step 7 to notice how your project impacts you now and is likely to influence your future. Look forward and consider your project with all your senses—visual, auditory, and kinesthetic. Additionally, continue other steps to fine-tune and enhance your life—reflect, ask for feedback from respected peers. Most of all, have fun!

A DEFINING MOMENT

These steps influence one another, so adjust them according to your circumstances. You might not do them in this order, but they are all essential and many will be repeated. This isn't a linear process; it's one you can tailor for yourself.

....
THE FAB FOUR RETURN

As promised in the Introduction, there truly are four knock-your-socks-off benefits to a 2% Project. But you need to implement the 10 steps previously discussed to get the big payoff. These "fab four" can provide incentives as you dig into your calendar to find time to invest in yourself. They'll help you answer the WIIFM question—What's In It For Me?

1. *Zest Appeal.* When you live from the zest of Esprit d'Core, you give your life the fullness and happiness that spontaneously flows from being committed to giving a voice to your inner wisdom.

2. *Congruency.* When you align your values with your daily living, there is true internal accountability, which creates authentic living that arises out of deep and honest personal reflection. It doesn't have to take a lot of time, but it does have to be honest.

3. *Identity.* When your identity is centered on your internal truth, you don't lose your bearings when normal lifecycle losses come your way. By learning to cope when you lose your outer labels, you know who you really are, without a photo ID.

4. *Passionate Equilibrium.* When you feel your passion for life renewing your world with balance and grace, you know you're living with passionate equilibrium.

As I've lived my 2% Solution, I've found it makes a difference in every part of my life. I have always had a tendency to focus on work and lose sight of my other joys. Throughout the 2% Process, I have improved my balance so I enjoy all aspects of my life, not just one. As a result, my spiritual growth is stronger, my relationships with my family and friends are more resilient and authentic, and my work is clearer and more real than ever. You will find that as you progress through your 2% Process, each one of these benefits will unfold for you.

. . . .

THE FINE PRINT: RULES OF ENGAGEMENT

It is true—implementing your 2% Project will liberate new life potential. However, it doesn't happen just by wishing or agreeing with the concept. I have given you fair warning that a good deal of hard work and commitment is involved. You will experience the results by digging in and doing the honest work of learning about yourself, listening to your heart, giving a voice to your wisdom, and practicing a consistent engagement with your plan. There aren't a lot of rules for reaping these benefits, but following each one of these rules of engagement is essential:

1. *Length of implementation.* You are working on making behavioral changes and creating a new alignment in your life. This takes time and practice. Commit to implementing your 2% Project for at least six months. Anticipate that it will influence your life permanently!

2. *Be honest and ask yourself probing questions.* This is a learning opportunity and you will reap benefits in proportion to your truthfulness with yourself. Apply the process of conscious self-awareness, which is described more fully in Chapter 4.

3. *Whenever possible, ask others for feedback.* Seek out people you believe will be honest and caring with you and ask them to tell you what they are noticing as you execute your 2% Process. You will find more about this rule in the 10-Step Action Plan.

Activity: *Developing Your 2% Solution and 2% Project*
Chapter 1 introduced the definitions of *2% Solution* and *2% Project*. Here, you will see more clearly how the two intersect to bring about transformative results in your life.

Think of your 2% Solution as your big picture goal. For example, your 2% Solution might be to bring art into your life. So how will you realize that goal? That's where your 2% Project comes in. Your first 2% Project might be to paint with watercolors for 30 minutes every day. At another stage of your life you may have a 2% Project focused on working with clay. Both of these bring you to your ultimate goal—your 2% Solution.

Take a first try at articulating your big picture goal.

My 2% Solution might be

_____

_____

_____

Refine this over time as you gain clarity on what you really want.

Your 2% Project will be a reflection and application of your personal values. Choosing your 2% Project is not necessarily any easier than choosing your 2% Solution, but at least you can break it down into smaller pieces. Remember, your 2% Project will help you achieve your powerful lifelong purpose. This is a valuable, fun, and profound opportunity, so make your decision carefully. Follow a process of combining your intuitive awareness and rational analysis skills in deciding on your 2% Project. You will continue fine-tuning these skills as you work through the strategies in this book.

First, start with some initial impressions. If you believe you know right away what your project ought to be, write it down.

My 2% Project might be

_____

_____

_____

If you're not so sure, or if you are interested in thinking it through more deeply, follow this meditative exercise.

1. Give yourself 10 undisturbed minutes or more to sit comfortably with your eyes closed, breathing deeply.

2. Ask yourself, "What is the most valuable *opportunity* I want in my life or one that I have but which I'm neglecting?" It should be an opportunity that, if addressed, will make an important difference in your life. You'll feel more aligned and great relief because you are doing something that feels authentic—something that really reflects *you*.

3. With your eyes still closed, ask your highest potential, your spirit, your soul, your best self how to accurately define your 2% Project.

4. Open your eyes, feel grateful for the connection with your wisdom, and then write notes about what came to you.

At this point you have one or two drafts of the core statement of your 2% Project. You might be exploring this topic for quite a while yet; it may take a few days or a month or more to be certain of your first 2% Project. Remember, this is about the quality and depth of your life, not rushing to achieve just one more thing.

Now that you understand the basics of the 10-Step Action Plan, it's time to see how it works. Try the following activity to help you create a structure for the next step. Fill in your answers to these questions or record them in your 2% Journal.

Here's a heads up as you work with the sample plan, one more step will be added in Chapter 4, so use that form as your ultimate guide.

Activity: *My 2% Action Plan*

1. My 2% Project is (remember, this will come with time and reflection):

2. I recognize that specific action is important, so I will set specific times for my project (list the day and hour when you'll work on your 2% Project and what you'll do):

   Day   **Time**   **Action**
   Monday

   Tuesday

   Wednesday

   Thursday

   Friday

   Saturday

   Sunday

   Or you might want a weekly format:
   Week 1 I will (fill in the dates and actions for the first week):

   Week 2 I will (continue this throughout your project):

3. Tools or other support items I need are:

4. My support team (name the people who will support you in accomplishing your goals, people who know you well enough to give you meaningful and considerate feedback):

5. My goals:
   • My goals for the first month are:
   • My goals for the first six months are:

> 6. How I will know that I'm on track to implementing my 2% Project:

VALUES—IDENTIFYING YOUR CORE BELIEFS

I appreciate the clarity of this quote and the strength of its opening: "Value is the life-giving power of anything." True. What gives your life power? So often in the busy, frantic world we inhabit, we operate on automatic pilot. We are caught in the hum of business that has us running from one task to another, and too often we don't even take time to notice why or if the task is useful, enjoyable, or fulfilling. Your 2% Project/Solution must reflect your values for you to form the commitment it takes to gain all your potential benefits. Each person's will differ—it could be engaging in ongoing learning, following a path of healthy living, or spending family time together.

> Value is the life-giving power of anything;
> Cost, the quantity of labor required to produce it;
> Price, the quantity of labor which its possessor will take in exchange for it.
>
> —John Ruskin, *Munera Pulveris* (1862)

In *The Power of Now*, Eckhart Tolle says that we normally live in "ordinary unconsciousness" (1997, 60). He is talking about operating in a fog without truly paying attention. I agree. It takes our personal intervention to be present and to live with awareness. Implementing a 2% Project causes your moment-to-moment awareness of life to converge with what truly matters to you. This can happen if you use the reflection and feedback processes incorporated in the 10-Step Action

Plan to help you hold yourself accountable and calibrate how close you are coming to success. You will define your own success to reflect your targets.

Without doubt, a life well lived requires sensitivity and awareness. You know you are living fully when your values are congruent with the way you live. You begin by taking responsibility for your life. There are always reasons everyone does what they do; at some level there are always choices. Of course, they are choices deeply influenced by our life conditions. Abraham Maslow, a 20th-century psychologist, developed what is known as a hierarchy of needs that demonstrates how choices are influenced in fundamental ways. Securing food and shelter are a primary need, followed by successive, higher-order ones, with self-actualization at the very top.

For those of us blessed to have so many of our basic needs satisfied, it is hard to believe that anyone can act like a victim. Yet, just about all of us—myself included—have played the victim role, at least in our thinking process. That thinking is one of the most profound ways to sabotage happiness. All too often we go through life moaning and groaning about our life conditions. It may be family commitments that weigh us down or work tasks that seem pointless; there are many ways to fill in the blank with complaints. When I catch myself doing this, I do my best to employ this four-step process:

1. Reaffirm my intent to live a life without internal complaints polluting my thinking and emotions.

2. Notice when I am complaining or acting in my thinking like I'm a victim of my world.

3. Change my thinking by interrupting with positive thoughts.

4. Accept without blaming myself that I had the thoughts, breathe, and be grateful for choosing to take whatever action I currently am taking. Remind myself that mistakes require correction, not punishment.

When we are conscious of our values, it is much easier to be aware of the life-giving power they hold, rather than the life-sucking drain of the tasks we undertake. Anytime you are feeling drained and that life is being sucked from you, remember that you have the opportunity to change your thinking. Use the four-step process I just described to give your life a power boost.

A DEFINING MOMENT

Over time, you may choose to have several 2% Projects—though one at a time. The cumulative benefit of your 2% Projects is the 2% Solution to your life. You are likely to find this leads you to a life well lived—on purpose!

Awareness also requires that we frequently clarify our values. Authentic human values are like instincts that radiate from our core, and they change as we evolve and grow strong enough to require more of ourselves. However, the ways in which we live our values is likely to fluctuate given our life conditions. When we experience a value shift, it may be because we have finally experienced the implementation of a value so thoroughly that we now see through new eyes. Be aware of your values and regularly check in with yourself to evaluate how congruently your life expresses them. The potency of the 2% Solution is that it brings a deeply held core value, lodged in the quiet of your soul, into active expression in your life. That is what makes it critical to reassess your values as you select your 2% Project and design your implementation plan. Do this quick perusal of your values to take inventory.

Activity: A Bird's-eye View of Your Values

1. Take some time to be calm and open your mind.

2. Write a list of your top six values in your 2% Journal (if suggestions will help, look at the following list).

3. Now think of yourself as an eagle flying over your life, and notice how you're living. Where are you spending your time? From that perspective, what would the eagle say your values are? List up to six.

4. Compare the two lists. Are they the same or different? Write about your observations.

Here's another way to clarify your values. This sorting process will help you clarify what is truly most important out of a cluster of values.

1. Look at the following list of potential values and notice if there are others of more importance to you.

2. Add in topics important to you that aren't listed.

3. Rate the importance of each one on a scale of 1 to 10, 10 being the most important for you.

4. Put a star by each attribute that is critical for you *at this point in your life.*

____ Telling the truth
____ Being kind to others
____ Responding to family needs
____ Developing professionally
____ Expanding your religious/spiritual practice
____ Learning more about a specific topic
____ Continuing your education
____ Giving your gifts to the world
____ Living a balanced lifestyle
____ Having fun
____ Engaging in civic activities
____ Contributing to your community
____ Supporting the arts
____ Staying healthy
____ Being respected by others
____ Other _____

Incorporate this information on your values clarification into the core statement of your 2% Project. A score of 8 to 10 and/or a star are good indicators that the value may be important to your project. List those values in your 2% Journal that are the most essential and should be supported and developed in your 2% Project:

My Core Values

The values I have given eight or more points are:

The values I starred as most critical for me right now are:

How am I addressing my critical values in my 2% Project?

Bonnie, whose story you read at the beginning of this chapter, described her key values as responding to family needs, developing and maintaining truthful intimate relationships, giving her gifts to the world, and living a balanced lifestyle. Developing her career was also important, but not as significant to her as the other values.

THE VALUE OF SPIRAL DYNAMICS

An extraordinary system that adds a new frame to understanding values is known as *Spiral Dynamics integral* (*SDi*). This system categorizes human values into eight levels of expression that reflect how our life conditions motivate us and determine what is important to us.

Humans must prepare for a momentous leap… It is not merely a transition to a new level of existence but the start of a new movement in the symphony of human history.

—Clare W. Graves

This system of thought is a tool that can help you pinpoint the best 2% Project to support the development of your values.

The SDi value system describes how a person thinks, not what is valued. People value different things because they think in different ways. Each value system can be considered its own container that holds a particular structure for thinking; each is a decision-making system for choosing what matters in life. The *i* in SDi stands for *integral* and is based on the premise that we are best off when we manage to integrate all the pieces together in our life work. You can learn more from the book *Spiral Dynamics* by Don Beck and Christopher Cowan (1996) and in the Resources section at the back of this book.

The theory of Spiral Dynamics was developed by Dr. Clare Graves, who emphasized that each world view is the developmental consequence of all previous learning. Don Beck, now the lead developer of Spiral Dynamics integral, writes on his website (www.spiraldynamics.net) that "By exploring and describing the core intelligences and deep values that flow beneath what we believe and do, the model offers a profoundly incisive, dynamic perspective on complex matters such as:

- HOW people think *about* things (as opposed to 'what' they think)

- WHY people make decisions in different ways

- WHY people respond to different motivators

- WHY and HOW values arise and spread

- The nature of CHANGE"

No one value system is intrinsically better than another; they just appear at different points in human development (both collectively and individually). We all are likely to experience changes in our value systems as our life conditions change. We all have some energy in several of the areas, and changing needs will drive us to evolve as we tackle different, tougher and more complex problems. The key tenet of Spiral Dynamics is to recognize that everyone is motivated, but that we aren't all motivated by the same things. Recognizing this can help you excel with your 2% initiative. Find what motivates you and understand how; then you can use that power to achieve your goal.

According to Spiral Dynamics, we all have a blend of eight world-views, so you will probably find you resonate with several of these sectors. See if you can find the one where your center of gravity rests—the one that feels most like home to you—and then use that to guide where you would place your 2% Project. The five levels most likely to influence you are discussed more fully below.

Blue is for people who are motivated to find purpose in living. If this is of central importance for you, you will like the order and clarity rules provide and believe they ought to be enforced. Deferring gratification, such as working hard now for a promotion later, feels good and right to you.

Orange is often thought of as the home of people with a strong entrepreneurial spirit. If this value cluster drives your goals and strategies, you are likely to "strive for autonomy and independence" and seek the material abundance that leads to the good life. You are likely to have a strong competitive spirit.

Green is the home of people with deep commitments to the kinds of causes that further justice and human equality, environmental protection, and animal rights. If

> It's simply that we have to awaken new ways of thinking.
>
> —Dr. Don Beck

this is you, you are likely strongly committed to your group identity, cooperation instead of competition, consensus decision-making, and expanded harmony.

Yellow initiates a very new way of thinking according to Graves. From this level on, you can see and appreciate the people and points of view expressed at the other levels of the spiral, even if you don't agree that the choices are the best ones which can be made. Key characteristics associated with this thought system include a focus on being flexible, fluid and competent. If this calls you, you will prefer integrated and open systems for communicating with others, for operating your business, and for conducting all your affairs.

Turquoise is populated by those who seek planetary renewal that includes and benefits everyone at all levels. Folks operating from this worldview embrace a collective global view and seek to consider all the potential consequences in critical decisions. If these values inspire your actions, you likely want to live sustainably and are committed to acting from a holistic perspective.

Source: Printed with permission by Don Beck, Ph. D.

Now take this system and apply it to your 2% Project. Gauge where you stand on the Spiral Dynamics scale currently, and from this model's point of view contemplate what is important for you to develop now. Because this system also does an excellent job in explaining the process of change, it can help you define your 2% Project and develop an implementation plan to realize the aspirations calling you.

As you consider where you fit in, you're likely to find parts that are unquestionably part of who you are, and probably parts that are itchy and scratchy, which you are chaffing against. Should your project help you explore this scratchiness? Do you need to change in response to the scratchiness or to solidify your core parts? Only you know the answer. It is important to consider the direction that will best support your growth so you can delve into the area that best supports your life's 2% Solution.

The following 2% in Motion story puts this theory into practice.

2% in Motion

ANN HITS A HIGH NOTE

Ann, a young mother and successful middle-management professional in a manufacturing company, described her 2% Project as "to return to my musical roots and share myself with my community through my flute playing." It meant some big changes for her. She said, "My family joined a church, I joined a wind ensemble associated with the church and played in some concerts and special music events." She has been implementing her 2% Project for several years and now describes it as "ongoing, but not to the extent that it was, due to my travel demands. We are more involved in our church than ever, and I have also returned to my piano playing and sharing with my daughter as she learns the piano."

Ann took the Spiral Dynamics measure and found she has considerable preference for two areas: blue and orange. At first, both of these preferences were expressed through putting much of her energy into developing her career, which met her needs in the orange entrepreneurial area. Furthermore, her company is straightforward and rules-oriented, which places it solidly in the blue arena. Her blue self was quite comfortable with the rules-oriented culture. However, she was not meeting other strong callings.

Her 2% Project has made a surprising and transformative difference in her professional development. She emphasizes with gusto that she's become much more assertive at work. Her boundaries are clearer. Because she clarified her values, she was able to determine her priorities. Ann wanted to diversify her life, adding in more of the energy. Music, family, and community are central to Ann, and so she is no longer willing to sacrifice those for the sake of work and growing her career.

Many of her blue values had been sacrificed to the orange corporate work world. By diversifying and balancing her life, everything worked better, and Ann became a much happier person. The result: more respect at work, a promotion, and more peace of mind. Sweet music, indeed! %

Engage Your EQ: *Assertiveness*

You'll recall from the Introduction and Chapter 1 that emotional intelligence skills are integral to a successful 2% Solution. A balanced expression of assertiveness, one of the EQ competencies, will help you find time for this new investment in yourself and spend your precious resources wisely.

Carving out time for yourself requires that you be assertive on your own behalf and that of others on important matters in a way that listeners feel respected. Your listeners need to believe they have the right and the ability to disagree with you. This constructive back-and-forth dynamic creates a positive atmosphere for dialogue and engagement.

I work with a wide diversity of groups and individuals, and I am always struck that over 75 percent of the people in a room usually raise their hands when I ask how many struggle with assertiveness. More women raise their hands than men, which I expect, but many men raise their hands as well. So why is using this skill so challenging? It is at the core of respectful and effective communications, and it is enormously influenced by cultural contexts. Assertiveness is contextualized by different cultures: you may be expected to behave a certain way at work, yet another way with your extended family, and still another at public meetings in your community. People can change jobs and start receiving criticism for communicating in a way that was not only acceptable but expected in their previous jobs.

Fortunately, a few key strategies will make a big difference in your use of this skill. Here are some pointers:

- First and foremost, *do* use this skill of assertiveness; otherwise, you won't be able to fulfill your life dreams and others will be deprived of your wisdom.

- Watch your tone when you speak. At its best, it should be inviting; at its worst, it should be neutral. Avoid being confrontational or condescending.

- Take ownership of the fact that this is your opinion or your need. Don't blame or act like a victim. Leave room for others to express their opinions and acknowledge that they see the situation differently.

The initial act of insisting on time for yourself to implement your 2% Project will often require that you be assertive. If you are interested in developing your assertiveness, you might consider working with a coach or taking a class at a local adult learning center.

TUNE IN YOUR MIND

- Write down your 2% Project again and contemplate your 10-Step Action Plan. Where are you going from here?

- Your 2% Project should amplify your core values. Make sure it does by going back to the values questionnaire and apply what you have learned to your project design. Spiral Dynamics will help you apply that information to guide your project.

- Assert yourself—you deserve to take 2% of your time for yourself! Consciously practice and enhance your assertiveness skills, keeping in mind that assertiveness is not synonymous with aggressiveness. Assertiveness means being sensitive to others while standing your ground.

TUNE OUT THE NOISE

- Your project is to satisfy a vital heart's desire; don't go for an easy out or what others say you should do.

- Pause and consider rather than rushing into the wrong project. Take time to think things through.

- Avoid the trap of thinking you don't have time for yourself. You don't have time *not* to invest in yourself!

A SNEAK PREVIEW

Some neuroscientists assert that seeing is believing. So be optimistic—see the best! In the next chapter you will learn to capitalize on your strengths and soar with them to achieve authentic success. This will be supported by developing the important emotional intelligence skill of optimism.

3/

EXPERIENCE THE "AH-HA"
Parlaying Strengths into Success

*E*mily tapped her fingers on her desk, but that did nothing to relieve her agitation. She tried pacing around her substantial office, looking out at the view. She was restless, even bored. She was the CEO of her own corporate training company, but she was unimpressed with herself. She was 48 years old and the World Trade Center buildings had just fallen. With this, she'd discovered life wasn't about the title, the office, or any of the other perks. Those were all fine, but that wasn't what made her tick. Yet she worried about whom she would be in the world if she left her own successful company. Still, she was bored and boredom was something she couldn't abide.

Emily, being her determined self, plowed ahead. She needed something new and she was motivated, outcome-oriented, and self-disciplined to seek it out. And why not? Emily has guts. Not too many people have the courage to let go of a high-paying, prestigious sure thing in an economic downturn. Nonetheless, she implemented her 2% Project with the same panache she did everything else.

She built a remarkable new business from her corporate training experience and her passion for nonprofits. She is a much sought-

after coach, working with big-hearted people who have underdeveloped business acumen. She helps nonprofits become stronger businesses, giving them tools, systems, and coaching that improve processes and enhance their long-term viability so they can continue to fulfill their missions.

Emily doubled her income the second year over her first year earnings as a coach and created numerous opportunities for congruent growth. Two years into her new career Emily is sailing! She recently presented her work at an international conference on coaching. And now she chooses only those clients whose mission she wants to support. Emily reports that her benefits from her 2% Project are "huge, as it is integrating my talents, desires, and strengths."

Emily capitalized on her strengths of motivation and action, self-discipline, and personal values to move toward one of the most all-encompassing strengths—self-actualization. As she focused on her 2% Project and used it to navigate through a major life change, her self-knowledge regarding her talents and skills helped her become more complete and self-actualized. %

Operating from your strengths is a concept that holds great hope: when you pay more attention to enhancing your strengths and place less emphasis on improving weaknesses, you will be increasingly successful. However, to fully capitalize on this practice, some balance is required. It's still essential to understand where your weaknesses, or challenge points, are creating a drag on your strengths; it's wise to use your strongest capabilities to modify your weaknesses.

Using strengths to achieve authentic success means tapping into your natural power. Increasing your emotional intelligence is a key factor in pumping up your strengths. Happiness and optimism, both components of EQ, are vital to true success; if you can enhance those aspects of your emotional intelligence, you will be well on your way toward authentic success. We'll explore optimism in this chapter and happiness in Chapter 5. Remember, unlike IQ, which you acquire from your genetic makeup, emotional intelligence can be learned, so it is vital to learn the concepts and practice them regularly.

> **A DEFINING MOMENT**
>
> The word **strength** has several meanings. In its first set of definitions, *Webster's* dictionary begins with "moral courage" such as "the inner strength of self-restraint" and moves on to physical strength and then to "the ability to produce an effect"—to influence. The second set of definitions begins with "a strong attribute or inherent asset." Each of these definitions brings richness to the full concept. Power is related to strength—putting *power* together with *strength* expands its meanings and creates an effective outcome for most people seeking to make a meaningful mark in their world.

Authentic success combines your inner and outer strengths, though integrating these two is not always so easy. Ideas for accomplishing that integration are included throughout this chapter, including by learning from the stories of others.

ALIGNING WITH SELF

Emily, who you met at the beginning of this chapter, went through an identity crisis when she decided to leave her life as the CEO of a corporate training company. This was her third career change. She often wondered if she would ever settle down. Perhaps she was a no-mad at heart, or perhaps she hadn't aligned herself with her essential Esprit d'Core. The only way to find out was to embrace this identity crisis; only by going deeper into herself could Emily find out who she really was.

When you are aligned with your core self, fear dissipates. Fear often comes from the uncertainty around conflicting goals and the concern about disagreeing with someone else. As you live more authentically, your confidence blooms and you are able to negotiate conflict much better because your Esprit d'Core provides the guiding light.

Most people are drawn to domains that draw on their strengths. When that happens, it fits so naturally that you are already in the flow—that state of total absorption and satisfaction that makes you oblivious to all else. When Michael Jordan plays basketball, the natural flow of his talents and strengths are true poetry in motion. He turns basketball into a dance. Rock stars, from Buddy Holly to the Beatles to the new generation of idols, leapt into their professions because they couldn't *not sing* and perform. Firing up your strengths gives you more fuel so you can operate on all cylinders. Tapping into strengths and putting them to work increases your effectiveness and allows you to fully use your gifts.

You may feel that you ended up in your profession because of the forces of gravity. That *could* be a good thing. Following gravity, as water does, will connect you with your natural flow. That's how the universe works. Of course, anyone can foul up the natural flow. You can over-analyze a situation, be frozen by paralysis, or let others' expectations drive your choices. The important question to ask is, "Am I operating with my strengths fully committed?" You will feel more authentically successful if you can answer "Yes."

Strengths have common characteristics. When you involve any particular strength, you are likely to feel like one or more of these:

- **The Pied Piper:** You talk; people listen. You are influential.

- **Ben Franklin:** You are comfortable acting from your strengths; the familiarity of it lets you act with confidence and authority.

- **Tiger Woods:** You are in the flow; there is nothing else but you, fully immersed in the moment.

- **Mae West:** You express a strong attribute or inherent asset fully, in your own style.

- **Dorothy in the Ruby Slippers:** You emanate power that comes from within; that power is stronger and more authentic than the power demonstrated by the Wizard of Oz before he was unmasked. Real power comes from your core strengths and your values.

It's great fun to employ your strengths, and it's even better when you focus on *expanding* your strengths and bringing these characteristics into your life more fully.

Franklin Delano Roosevelt, the thirty-second president of the United States, is an excellent example of someone who excelled at expanding strengths. He was one of the most powerful leaders the U.S. has ever experienced. FDR took the nation out of the Depression, rebuilt jobs, and led a war-weary nation back into the world theater of war when he saw the indisputable necessity of American involvement to protect freedom. He couldn't have been a legendary leader if he hadn't been in the flow. He was in the right job: the one for which he had trained, which called for his powers of oratory, courage, and insightfulness. He exercised his strong attributes and inherent assets, displaying strengths central to leading his country through deeply troubled times. FDR brought all the characteristics of strength listed earlier to life for himself and his nation.

Your challenges may be somewhat different, but in this fast-paced world there is no debating the need for courage. Without courage it is difficult to make choices that have a positive effect in the world. You can apply that courage best in the areas of your own strengths.

KNOWING YOUR STRENGTHS

To learn about your own strengths, tune in to your best guidance: your own inner wisdom. Take time and give yourself the gift of thoughtfully filling in the "My Strengths" survey. Don't worry about getting it right; this self-assessment is an opportunity to expand your awareness. If you are honest, you will be right. Pay attention to doing this exercise just for yourself; you don't need to worry about being judged or impressing anyone. As you think about each topic in the survey, consider your subjective point of view and also how those who know you best see you.

Activity: *My Strengths*

- I define personal strengths as:
- My five key strengths are:
    1.
    2.
    3.

4.

5.

- How do I know these are my strengths? When I'm using these skills, what do I feel, produce, employ?

- Am I bringing these strengths to life? Does my work center on them?

- How does my 2% Project support the application of my strengths?

2% in Motion

COMING UP FOR AIR

Ruth joined a women's leadership group and began to realize she needed to make a change. She thoughtfully reported, "I was physically, emotionally, and spiritually sick—I was spiraling downward and out of control. I had to do something. I had been journaling for some time, but then I never read my notes. One of my leaders challenged me to read what I wrote so I could learn about myself. I was flying from Phoenix to Denver, and I decided to read my journal. As I noticed a recurring theme of not being happy with myself, I had an anxiety attack. I ended up in the bathroom on the airplane, sobbing for about 15 minutes. I knew that I had to do something."

Today, Ruth is a different person. She is enthusiastic, congruent with herself, and much happier. Her 2% Project was about rediscovering who she is and then accepting and loving herself. She continued, "My initial objective was to be more accepting of others—since I was usually perfect! If I could accept their faults, everything would be OK. About halfway through my project in my leadership program, I finally got it! What I really needed to do was to accept myself. My perfectionism had been caused by my own fear of failure or rejection—it never was about them! In addition, at the beginning of the program I had just been diagnosed with MS and was in denial big-time, and angry."

It took some time and support for Ruth to learn to love herself, but she got there. Because of her project, Ruth learned how to dismantle her perfectionism. She created a life that honors her whole self. She retooled for daily living so that it is congruent with her Esprit d'Core. She honors her body and its needs and no longer overstresses it. The benefits for Ruth, her family, and her colleagues are difficult to exaggerate. ☯

REDEFINING STRENGTHS

As previously noted, there are multiple ways to define strengths. In *Authentic Happiness,* Martin Seligman reports on the survey he co-directed with Chris Peterson at the Values in Action Institute (VIA). He paints a very different picture of strengths from the one the Gallup Organization presents, as described in *Now, Discover Your Strengths* by Marcus Buckingham and Donald Clifton. At Collaborative Growth, we view strengths through an even larger lens as we bring together the three-part harmony of building on strengths, managing weaknesses, and building emotional intelligence.

One common feature among the VIA, Gallup, and Collaborative Growth approaches is recommending that you work from your strengths, using these core assets to support your skills. Our differences come in the attention given to weaknesses and in what is considered a strength.

The VIA Institute: Improve Traits to Boost Strengths

Seligman and Petersen thought it was important to understand what constitutes good character. They began by identifying the virtues that have shown up in most cultures and traditions. Seligman in *Authentic Happiness* (132) describes the effort this way:

"Led by Katherine Dahlsgaard, we read Aristotle and Plato, Aquinas and Augustine, the Old Testament and the Talmud, Confucius, Buddha, Lao-Tze, Bushido (the samurai code), the Koran, Benjamin Franklin, and the Upanishads—some two hundred virtue catalogues in all. To our surprise, almost every single one of these traditions flung across three thousand years and the entire face of the earth endorsed six virtues:

- Wisdom and knowledge

- Courage

- Love and humanity

- Justice

- Temperance

- Spirituality and transcendence"

The VIA authors identified 24 paths to accomplish these six virtues. Each of the 24 paths represents a strength—a trait—in action. A *trait* is a behavior you use in many situations, such as consistent kindness. Importantly, a trait can be enhanced; it may take hard work, but you can grow any strength that is important to you.

A DEFINING MOMENT

Traits, such as curiosity about the world and love of learning, are distinguished from **talents**, which are probably genetically hardwired, such as perfect pitch or the ability to be a classic ballerina. You can grow a trait, but talents are pretty much fixed. According to the VIA our traits are our strengths.

Traits are morally important capabilities related to the exercise of the six virtues; talents are morally neutral. According to the VIA, traits are displayed consistently over time. A trait/strength is useful—for example, practical intelligence or street smarts—and is something families wish for their loved ones. As I write this, my grandnephew, Landen, was born just a few hours ago. Without a doubt, his loving parents and our large extended family pray that he will have the traits and virtues identified by the VIA authors—for instance, the traits of perseverance, honesty, and social intelligence.

Seligman calls for using our signature strengths every day and in all parts of our lives and believes this will bring us abundant gratification and authentic happiness. His suggestions for using your signature strengths come close to the strategies Collaborative Growth recommends for your 2% Process, but there are differences as well, as you will see.

Gallup: Improve Talent to Boost Strengths

The Gallup approach to strengths is quite different from the VIA method: because of its focus on morally neutral *talents as our strengths*, though there is some crossover. Gallup defines strength as "consistent near-perfect performance in an activity" (25). Tiger Woods' exceptional golfing skill is their number one example. Gallup believes your strengths are recurring patterns created by connections in your brain that can be productively applied. However, their description of how the brain operates is much more limited than others believe. They argue essentially that we should identify our innate talents and keep growing them because learning new ways of behaving is nearly hopeless. The Gallup approach is described in *Now, Discover Your Strengths* by Buckingham and Clifton—a work that claims we learn most of what we are going to learn by the time we are three years old. Many, including me, disagree with this dire conclusion.

In contrast, Fred Gage, the 2002 president of the Society for Neuroscience, explained the discovery of *neurogenesis*, the phenomenon of adult brains growing new neurons. These new neurons enable people to continue learning throughout their lives. The brain produces new nerve cells and can rewire itself in response to experience. ("Brain Repair Yourself," *Scientific American,* September 2003).

As complex beings, humans are a healthy combination of nature and nurture. This combination is also reflected in the work of experts in emotional intelligence, such as Daniel Goleman, Reuven Bar-On, Richard Boyatzis, and Annie McKee, as well as in Seligman's approach to strengths.

To learn and grow to your fullest capabilities, you must expand your strengths—and pay attention to modifying any behaviors that are a barrier to your success. Through my decades of work with individuals and teams, I have watched thousands of people grow and improve. I caution you to be careful about accepting any theory that holds once a weakness, always a weakness. The 2% method encourages us to be all we can be by using your strengths to overcome challenges.

The Collaborative Growth Trifecta: Strengths, Weaknesses, and EQ

At Collaborative Growth, we serve as strategic communications partners for people in all types of organizations. We have found that helping people recognize their strengths gives them the opportunity to celebrate their capabilities, use them wisely, and connect their actions with their skills.

Profound learning also happens as our clients are challenged to recognize and confront their weaknesses. They must notice the behaviors that limit their success. For example, we have worked with brilliant scientists who have much to contribute, but whose ignorance of social and emotional skills can be a powder keg. Some don't seem to grasp the antidiscrimination laws of the U.S. Civil Rights Act, and it creates tremendous tension and difficulties for them as well the agencies for which they work. When trained about the law and given the opportunity to learn the power of empathy, respect, and sensitivity, they can change their behavior. This type of transition happens repeatedly, and it is one of the most rewarding parts of my work.

We have more momentum, more natural success, available when we expand our strengths. In all probability, the calling in your heart that led to your 2% Project will cause you to enhance your strengths. Your project will likely be an area where you know you can be even better, where you have gifts you're hungry to share with the world, and this can naturally lead to success.

The best way to achieve authentic success is on the path created by your strengths. At Collaborative Growth, we work with these six areas of strengths:

1. Action and motivation

2. Knowledge

3. Self-discipline

4. Positive relationships

5. Personal values and social accountability

6. Self-actualization

For a snapshot of your own strengths, first look over the questionnaire below, and then go through it strength by strength. When you're through, review and score the list to see where your greatest strengths lie.

Activity: *Snapshot of My Strengths*

Instructions: Read through the definitions and questions in each of the six strengths and check the ones that apply to you. To indicate how strongly they describe you, write in a 5 for very much like me, 3 for like me, and 1 for occasionally like me.

Action and Motivation

Action and motivation are all about getting the job done! These combined strengths depend on the driving energy, intention, and goal orientation that completing a task and leading others requires. People with these strengths are likely to be focused, aware of future implications of their actions, and able to persevere in the face of challenges.

_____ I know when it is time to end a discussion, so I am the one who proposes decisive action.

_____ I feel comfortable saying no even when I really wish I could say yes.

_____ I am self-directed.

_____ I easily connect with new goals and move toward completing them.

_____ I have a sense of pride or joy when I'm focused on a key task.

Knowledge

Knowledge is a strength for those who love learning and applying new skills and information. People with this strength are curious, love to do research, apply street smarts, may read multiple books at a time, and are often described as analytical.

_____ Learning something new is always very exciting to me.

_____ I value my ability to think critically and use it a lot in my work.

_____ I check my observations when I encounter difficulties to make sure I'm perceiving things accurately.

_____ Every day I seek out opportunities to expand my skills and knowledge.

_____ I have a good imagination, but it doesn't make me lose sight of objective reality.

Self-Discipline

Self-discipline is a strength that helps you control impulsivity and impatience. It helps you restrain yourself and pay attention to your desires and to your intentions to get what you want. Self-disciplined people tend to plan effectively and see projects through to completion.

_____ Others have acknowledged me for my patience and tolerance.

_____ While I value my feelings, I choose the best way to express them.

_____ Delayed gratification is a strategy that pays off well for me.

_____ I believe that humility is important to my success.

_____ When I make a commitment, such as to exercise or follow a diet, I stick to it.

Positive Relationships

The strength to build and maintain good relationships emerges out of specific skills, attitudes, and behaviors. Communication, empathy, and respect for others are, for example, essential.

_____ I'm good at understanding and describing the feelings of others.

_____ I always do my best to connect with someone before I give them advice.

_____ It is important to me to notice other people's needs and to respond to those needs appropriately.

_____ I am willing to tell others how I feel.

_____ I consider the effects of my actions on others before I act.

Personal Values and Social Accountability

This realm of strength reflects how core values such as honesty, courage, optimism, and responsibility to others influence your decision-making. People with this strength are likely to be loyal to their organization or their profession, committed to teamwork, and to take time to think about the moral implications of their actions.

_____ Others depend on me to do the right thing.

_____ I always do my best to face my fears and stand up for my beliefs.

_____ Even when there are obstacles in my way, I finish what I start.

_____ I'm a truthful person and others know they can always trust me.

_____ Others often describe me as loyal and reliable.

Self-Actualization

Self-actualization is a strength that relies on your being happy with your life. It also requires that you have a sense of your capabilities and that you are on the path to fulfilling your purpose in life. Do you feel a meaningful sense of purpose? How does what you are doing fit into the long-term, big picture of your life? How does it relate to what you are doing today?

_____ I seem to naturally appreciate the beauty in life.

_____ I'm satisfied with my overall success in life even though I want to do more.

_____ There is a spiritual component to life that we often tend to overlook.

____ It is important for me to have a sense of purpose and to reward myself for accomplishing milestones along the way.

____ I focus on the possibilities of fulfilling my life's mission.

Instructions for scoring: Calculate your total score for each of the strengths areas and record them here.

____ Action and motivation

____ Knowledge

____ Self-discipline

____ Positive Relationships

____ Personal values and social accountability

____ Self-actualization

Look at the rank order of your particular scores to see what your strengths and stretches are. It's the scores per category and rank order you're looking for, not the total of all six categories. Take some time to evaluate areas that may create a drag on your success. Compare the "My Strengths" survey you filled out above to this "Snapshot of My Strengths" to see how they compare. What do you recognize about yourself? The next step is to connect your strengths with your 2% Project.

2% in Motion

MAN AGAINST MACHINE

As a young man, Pete served in the military maintaining electrical equipment. He had expected to succeed at this job quickly—but he didn't. He plugged along, getting the basics done, but something big was missing. Just as he began to wonder if he was as capable as he had assumed, he was reassigned as a recruiter. From that day on, Pete's life changed. He was happy, and he met both the military's and his own standards for success. Why? Pete's strengths are personal relationships, self-discipline, and social accountability. He loved hanging out with people, not machines. Pete brought his strengths to his recruiting job, and he was motivated by his belief that he was helping to make the world better, which filled his need for social accountability.

After Pete left the military, he established his own recruiting company. He began a 2% Project to give back to the community by making a difference in his local chamber of commerce and at his church.

When Pete aligned his strengths with his 2% Project, his analysis looked like this:

My Strengths and My 2% Project	
Strengths	**2% Project**
• Relationships • Optimism • Self-regard • Community awareness and concern	*Focus*: To use my skills in making a contribution to the community.
	Action Plan: Use my optimism and skills in relationships to • Work for the metropolitan chamber of commerce. This will make a positive difference in the business community. • Volunteer at church. This will make a positive difference for my family and community.
Other Reflections	
Watch as other strengths develop and use them. The biggest drag on my success is that I'd rather work with people than learn the facts and details. I'll pay attention to this challenge.	*Action Plan*: Set aside time to learn the details on a weekly basis and reward myself with a game of golf with business contacts afterwards.

LINKING STRENGTHS TO YOUR 2% PROJECT

If you haven't already selected your 2% Project, ask yourself whether this is the right time to bring it to life. The return on a 2% Project—the payoff—is so disproportionate to the investment you make that it's practically miraculous. Part of the reason that a small-time investment in the 2% Process packs so much punch is that it helps you recognize and harness your strengths so you can then apply that wisdom to the rest of your life. Pete certainly learned to recognize his strengths, and then he built a successful and happy career and life on that wisdom. You might make a chart like Pete's and note the strengths you want to use in your 2% Project. Keep these strengths in mind and refer to the chart as you continue to work your way through implementing the ten steps of your 2% Project.

Linking your 2% Project to your strengths will help you grow stronger. Moreover, it will teach you to apply your strengths in other assignments and projects you tackle. If a project isn't going anywhere, conduct an assessment like the one on Pete's chart. Does the job call you to act outside your strengths? Can you make changes? If an assignment at work is going remarkably smoothly, what are the connections with your strengths? Such awareness can make a considerable difference in your life. This is how you expand your 2% effect.

Engage Your EQ: _Optimism_

While happiness is a general sense of well-being, optimism is the ability to look at the brighter side of life even when things are challenging. In _The EQ Edge_, Steven Stein and Howard Book identify three challenges to optimism—permanence, pervasiveness, and personalizing.

It's all about how you manage your thinking. You are in charge of your thinking, even if you aren't paying attention to the messages you give yourself; that itself is a choice. Choosing an optimistic life is as positive a message as you can give yourself. I promise this is truly "the gift that keeps on giving." Optimistic people are more successful in their life goals.

Being optimistic has everything to do with how you frame events:

- You view a challenge as temporary. For example, you think, "I need to work late until this project is done" rather than, "I need to work late and that will just go on for my whole life."

- You identify a problem as a specific concern, not as the dominant factor in your life. For example, "I'm having trouble meeting my family obligations because of this new project, but if I really concentrate on it, we'll get it wrapped up soon," rather than, "I'm always too busy; I will continue to disappoint my family because I'll never be present."

- You take responsibility and don't feel victimized. For example, "I took on this project to advance my career, and the extra hours are worth it," rather than, "It's my bad luck to get an assignment that keeps me from having a life outside the office."

Aron Ralston exemplifies optimism. He is the climber who got trapped in a slot canyon in southern Utah and ended up cutting off his hand to save his life. His ability to be decisive and act is as inspirational and instructive as it gets. He was able to recognize his predicament as temporary, isolate the problem, and solve it, believing that the sacrifice was worth the reward. The beauty of this thought system is that it helps people believe and act as if they have some control over their lives; it lowers stress and promotes flexible thinking. This is a recipe for success whether you are seeking to save your life, as Aron was, or to be more productive or balanced at work and in life, as so many of us are.

Here are two ideas to use as you develop your 2% Solution:

1. Concentrate on the answer, not the problem. For instance, list the major factors in a problem you currently face. Now stand up, walk to a window and notice what is going on in nature, take a drink of water,

and then return and think about a solution. Consider all the possible ways that just might lead to a positive resolution. What skills can you bring to the challenge?

2. When you talk about a problem, talk about it as temporary, even if you don't know just how long "temporary" will be. Notice the skills you can bring to this.

Through your choice to engage with life optimistically or pessimistically, you color your world. Look around: Did you get the big box of 64 crayons out to color with, or are black and white predominating? Believe it or not, you'll have a lot more colors to create with if you entertain your curiosity and regularly take time for fun. Play hard, color wildly, and go outside the lines!

THE REAL MCCOY: AUTHENTIC SUCCESS

When your strengths are enhanced by happiness and optimism, you can obtain *authentic success*. Research demonstrates that being happy and viewing the events of life with optimism lead to more productivity and success. That is a very good thing when it's authentic. In truth, success may or may not be a good thing. For example, skyrocketing to be the top dog in a particular company or industry may be a very attractive goal, but many a CEO has gotten there only to be perfectly miserable because of the high price that has been paid. The stress and the hours may cost them good health and close family bonds—that's a harsh definition of success.

Authentic success begets peace of mind, because when you're in this zone, you are living and working in accord with your strengths instead of fighting or ignoring them. You are also acting in sync with your values. Thus, when I use *authentic* to qualify *success*, I am referring to success being a reflection of your values and your strengths. My business partner (who is also my husband) enjoyed an earlier career in the construction industry. He built homes and offices; he now applies that creative energy to building teams and helping individuals through coaching. At one time, he drew on his strength of creativity to visualize and construct buildings; now he draws on it to build relationships and emotional intelligence. I, too, love to be creative, but unlike my husband, I couldn't possibly build a house. Or, if somehow I did build one by dint of some absurd amount of determination, it would not be a happy process and it would not result in authentic success. Rather, it would be a demonstration of forced will.

Understanding success is complicated and highly personal. You have a great deal of control over your relationship with success "simply" by noticing the messages you give yourself. Here, *simply* does not imply easily! Mastering thoughts is one of the hardest jobs humans face. In the search to understand authentic success, you must first define your own meaning of success. Without careful inquiry, you are all too likely to fall into the trap reflected by a favorite warning I give my clients and colleagues:

Quit beating yourself up because you haven't done what you don't want to do.

How often have you thought over and over, "I have to earn more so I can travel/buy a boat/whatever?" Since you aren't earning that additional amount, does that mean you aren't successful? Challenge yourself on that thought. Perhaps you are doing tremendously rewarding work. Can you be grateful and value your current success while also seeking to grow?

Words associated with authentic are *genuine*, *veritable*, and *bona fide*. Authenticity involves fidelity and sincerity without pretense, hypocrisy, or massive struggle. In exploring the word, its value becomes more apparent.

Authenticity becomes even more valuable when linked with success. How do you know when you are truly successful? What is the difference between authentic success and success that costs too much? When you achieve true success, you begin acting with a natural rhythm.

A DEFINING MOMENT

You know you are experiencing authentic success when being and doing are united. It's like that great song from Frank Sinatra—do be do be do.

Discover how you envision success by taking the Success Quiz. This will help you gain a sense of what messages you give yourself regarding success.

Activity: *Success Quiz*

Put a check by each item that describes success for you. Then put a check by each item that describes values that are important to you. These questions are highly personal, so feel free to add other items to both lists so that they become fully descriptive for you.

Part I

Success	Values
___ Being happy	___ Being honest
___ Being healthy	___ Being kind and compassionate
___ Having money	___ Using your talents
___ Achieving your potential	___ Living a moral life
___ Having close friends	___Taking care of others
___ Being married or having a partner	___ Living a balanced life
___ Raising children	___ Learning
___ Having a rewarding career	___ Performing public services
___ Being able to travel	___ Having fun
___ Being respected	___ Praying
___ Having power and choice	___ Focusing on spiritual development
___ (insert your own)	___ (insert your own)
___ (insert your own)	___ (insert your own)

Part II

Go to a place where you won't be interrupted, a place that feels like a treat—perhaps a park or a coffee shop. Take enough time to really think about your responses in Part I. Then contemplate and write in your 2% Journal about these questions and others that come to you.

- How do these two lists fit together as you are living your life now?

- Do you have one great statement about success that sounds highly evolved, such as "Success is about the quality of time with my family and friends, and taking care of my health." Yet at the same time you often give yourself contradictory messages, such as "I just won't be successful until I earn more or get more recognition." If so, reflect on the differences of these messages. Now write your statement of success for yourself and put it up in a visible place where you will see it daily.

Connecting inner and outer success means having the wisdom and courage to incorporate your values in your definition of success. It also means regularly checking in to notice when you need to redefine success or challenge messages you are giving yourself. Just as we can drive ourselves crazy, we can pay attention to our inner needs and lead ourselves to authentic success by establishing harmony with our inner- and outer-selves. Use your 2% Process to bring your whole life to more authentic success.

Authentic Success Isn't Really Algebra!

$$2\% + S + A + EQ = AS$$

2% of your time devoted to your 2% project + understanding and using your **strengths** + **awareness** of the relationship between your 2% Solution and your strengths + applying your **EQ** (emotional quotient), particularly your happiness and optimism, is guaranteed to = **Authentic Success**.

Employ this formula, pay attention, play, and reflect, and as you find and use your strengths, you will find new worlds and possibilities opening for you. Don't expect your 2% Solution to just happen any more than authentic success will. Both need your careful awareness and considered attention. You will gain value in relation to your investment. You only need to put a limited amount of time into your project, but your activity must be wholeheartedly thought out and integrated with your strengths and your skills in emotional intelligence. It is in following this formula that you can gain so much benefit while spending such a small amount of your time.

TUNE IN YOUR MIND

- Follow the formula: $2\% + S + A + EQ = AS$

- Learn to recognize and build on your strengths; they are your areas of greatest flow and greatest power. At the same time, address your weaknesses and use your strengths to keep your problems from undermining your success.

- Cultivate optimism by reminding yourself that challenging situations are temporary and every problem has a solution, even if you aren't aware of it *yet*.

- Tie your 2% Project to your intention of creating authentic success in your life.

TUNE OUT THE NOISE

- Make sure your desire to be successful "by doing a great deal" is not sabotaging your happiness by making you tired and grouchy.

- Don't accept pessimism as a genetic trait. You really can grow your optimism and enjoy increased success.

- Don't get cavalier about your weaknesses. A major weakness can bring down your strengths.

- Avoid the trap of thinking that money equals success or that you can just take success for granted.

A SNEAK PREVIEW

Chapter 4 highlights strategies to promote self-awareness—being engaged means being awake to what is happening in your life. Reflective skills are the ticket to gaining this benefit, and you will learn how you can really benefit from taking advantage of a wide variety of reflective strategies.

4/

MIRROR, MIRROR
ON THE WALL
The Art of Self-Reflection

Terry was the kind of person other people want to emulate. She seemed to have all the luck—she was genuinely happy, well liked, and healthy. She enjoyed her job, her free time, and her family. She knew who she was and where she was going. All in all, life was pretty fine. Then the bottom dropped out so completely that it seemed like a bad movie. Her brother and dearest friend, Dave, died unexpectedly. Her husband relapsed into heavy drinking, which led to their divorce. Corporate re-engineering stranded her outside the doors of a company she had loved. Suddenly Terry went from knowing exactly who she was and what her life was about to having her personal identity dismantled. She lost the pivotal labels by which she recognized herself; no longer could she call herself sister, wife, or manager.

Terry began her 2% Project after the first blow—her brother's death. Her project slowly became self-evident—to redefine herself, internally. She committed 30 minutes a day to reflective practices, often journaling, other times talking with selected close friends. She continued the same process as her husband relapsed and sometimes traded attending an Al-Anon meeting with writing in her journal. She was so challenged that at times she chose to spend more than 30 minutes a day. The key is she regularly gave at least three and a half hours a week. When her job disappeared, she was ready to make big lifestyle changes and not return to work for awhile. She enjoyed the time off from work, made several trips to Ireland to discover her roots, and learned to live simply. She's chosen to expand her 2% time to a larger amount of her life because she has the available time and she's gaining immense value. %

Although humans are complex creatures, we often reduce ourselves to labels that define us in sound bytes. Holiday parties, back-to-school events, and social outings with new friends are always filled with the quick banter of people summing up their lives and passions into a two-minute spiel. This same fundamental sense of identity governs our choices, our sense of possibility. It's what keeps the quintessential tough guy from crying and polished, buttoned-down, briefcase-toting employees from being the entrepreneurs they are called to be instead of clinging to a safe salary. There can be no doubt that self-identity—the ways in which we characterize ourselves—deeply impacts how much we will risk in order to bring all of our gifts to life.

———————— o ————————

No matter how fast you run,
Your shadow more than keeps up.
Sometimes, it's in front!
Only full, overhead sun diminishes
  your shadow.
You must have shadow and light
  source both.
Listen, and lay your head under the
  tree of awe.

—Rumi
(Coleman Barks, *The Essential Rumi*)

———————— o ————————

WHO ARE YOU?

The answer to this question may seem obvious—but it may not be. It's vital that you understand your own essence, beyond the sound bytes you may use at a cocktail party. If you aren't sure about who you are, take time as you read this chapter and as you engage in your 2% Project to work with this invitation to self-inquiry. Without knowing yourself, you're lost, or at least wandering. Living a purposeful life requires having a sense of who you are so that you can make moral and motivating decisions in accordance with the core of your being.

Surprisingly, although this skill is the bedrock of full human functioning, many people need remedial training. In the frenzy of the 21st century, our culture rarely teaches or supports self-reflection. Children and adults often don't have the skills to create their own identities and to know themselves. Not surprisingly, the deluge of media that surrounds us has a powerful pull because so many people lack a strong sense of identity. The advertisers are having a field day!

One of the best strategies for understanding your identity, and being able to cope when it changes, is to adopt some powerful reflective tools, some metaphorical mirrors. Used well, these will guide you in embracing your true identity. In this chapter you will have the opportunity to:

- Dance the night away. Enhance your ability to articulate your sense of self by two-stepping with the question "Who am I?"

- Add some polish. Shine up your 2% Project so that you can see yourself reflected in the project because you understand yourself more intimately.

- Get bigger while leaving your waistline intact. Expand your EQ skills with self-regard.

- Go on a scavenger hunt. Explore various strategies for reflecting on and determining your preferred reflective style.

- Connect the dots. Link accountability and emotional intelligence to add horsepower to your 2% Project.

Of course, like any skill, self-inquiry can be used to an extreme. It can become its own end instead of a means to the end you are seeking. Endless contemplation can stall progress, keeping you from getting on with the miracle of life. Balance is the ticket; ask the question honestly, probe for all your information, listen well, and then act.

I encourage you to make good use of your 2% Journal as you do the activities in this chapter. Learning reflecting skills is like learning aikido, the tango, or meditation: reading can introduce the subject, but the true value comes from playing with it. Experiment to find your path.

Activity: *Discovering Who You Are*

1. Take time to clarify your sense of identity. Circle any of the following words that are central to understanding who you are.

Spouse	Officer/Manager	Community activist
Parent	Employee	Volunteer
Sibling	Professional	Athlete
Aunt/Uncle	Team member	Artisan (e.g., a quilter or potter)

    Now jot down in your 2% Journal what it is that makes you who you are. Answer questions such as the following:

    *   I am a __ year old woman/man with __ (list family relationships such as a spouse and children).

    *   I am a __ (list your profession if relevant), and then write something about who you are there.

    *   List how you strive to make a difference, what you are learning, and what your goals are. Describe your passion and what stretches you at work or in any other part of life that is critical for you.

2. Zero in on the truth, not the superficial cocktail conversation. Dig deep; don't settle for the sound byte. Your payoff is directly related to your investment. So, who are you? Write it here, or if you'd like more space, use your 2% Journal.

    I am. . . _____
    _____
    _____

REFLECT TO KNOW YOURSELF

"Who am I?" is a profound question. It strikes at the heart of why you are on this planet, what your responsibility is to yourself and others, and what your critical moral choices will be. It is a question addressed in many religious and spiritual contexts. Ramana Maharshi, a great Hindu teacher from India, focused his teaching on the practice of self-inquiry. In *Be As You Are* (1972), Maharshi teaches the process of asking ourselves who we are over and over until we finally get to our core.

Ramana and teachers who carry on his teaching today, such as Gangaji, emphasize the path to knowing our full self through a process which eventually takes us *out* of constantly focusing on ourselves. Deepak Chopra makes a similar point in *The Book of Secrets* (2004), as does Eckhart Tolle in *The Power of Now* (1999). This is a necessary progression. We must first develop a clear personal awareness before we can give it up. The developmental process is:

Being an unaware part of the masses, living our life on autopilot.

Being aware, living consciously, choosing deliberately.

Letting go of our personal story and our self-centered focus while still using our capability of awareness to choose our actions in accordance with our highest motivating source.

MY IDENTITY, MY CHOICES

Your sense of identity has a direct effect on the type of choices you make. Is it a unified theme in your life or is it generic such as your nationality: "I am Canadian or French or American"; or your religious or spiritual affiliation: "I am Catholic or Hindu or Muslim" or your career:

"I am a lawyer or accountant or a manager." Whatever you draw from in answering that pivotal question of *Who am I?* will guide your choices from the mundane to the sublime.

A DEFINING MOMENT

Webster's dictionary defines **identity** as "unity and persistence of personality; unity or individual comprehensiveness of a life or character." Alternatively, it is also defined as "the condition of being the same with something described, claimed, or asserted."

A successful professional may want a big house to demonstrate success, one where clients and colleagues can be properly entertained. If being a visibly successful professional and living simply are both important, it is likely that there will be a clash between seeking to fulfill that identity and living the value of simplicity. This is the type of challenge the 2% Process is designed to help you address.

Step 3 of the 10-Step Action Plan calls for you to use your reflective skills. This step helps you meet the goal of aligning with your Esprit d'Core and living in synch with your values. If you truly use the reflective process as part of your 2% Project to address any values conflicts you are struggling with and keep at it for six months or more, you are likely to learn a great deal, clarify your values, and move through many of your conflicts about your values and your identity. You may still experience challenges in your busy world, but you are likely to have increased peace of mind about your choices. Find a way to continually use your reflective skills to check out the congruence between your lifestyle and your values so that you establish a comprehensive 2% Solution.

Be aware that, as Terry in the opening story learned, to the extent that your identity is defined by external attributes—such as work, relationships, and objects—you are at risk of losing your life as you know it. Impermanence, as the Buddhists teach us, is the law of the land. Your ability to adapt to change is one of the most helpful skills you can learn; it will support your desire to bring your gifts to the table of life.

2% in Motion

RECLAIMING A LOST CHILD

Theresa had plenty of good reasons to disconnect from herself. She was a survivor of childhood sexual abuse. Though that disconnect from the world served her as a survival skill to overcome the heinous crimes she experienced, that continued disconnect as an adult was causing her life to unravel. Often the very same skills that help a child survive can wreak havoc when that child becomes an adult.

Theresa was desperate to connect the dots and operate from a fully integrated sense of self. Her life and her relationships were suffering. Theresa took on a 2% Project of writing about her childhood sexual abuse. It was both undeniably hard and yet freeing. So she wrote and wrote, peeling back the layers of painful memories she had buried in the past. Theresa came to know faces of herself that had been far too painful to confront until now. She expanded her project by seeing a therapist and joining a support group. Finally, she was able to integrate her child self and her adult self. She was able to love herself—her little girl self—in a primal way that had been stripped from her and taken without her permission. She was able to reclaim her lost child, mother herself, and know that she is no longer a powerless little girl who is without resources or succor. The adult Theresa is now in charge, and she will always protect that child within.

She has awakened long-dead parts of herself and reclaimed territory that she'd surrendered in her fight for survival. She is more in touch with herself, and that has also caused her to be more connected globally. Theresa describes the 2% Process as "finding the small crack in the window of your life and letting the window open wider to let in fresher air." Today, Theresa is breathing easier with the abundance of fresh air in her life. %

LIVE WITH INTENTION, STAND AT ATTENTION

In one facet of my work as a consultant, I provide training for many types of groups in a variety of settings, from senior executives in large corporations to teams in our local zoning and planning departments.

I have found that people stay focused better and are more likely to re-
tain what they learn if I ask at the beginning of our work together for
them to take some reflective time and write down their intentions for
participating.

This also works well for executive coaching and for me personally.
We become fully present when we use the power of self-awareness to
reap the full value of our investment. Committing something to paper
or computer screen is a powerful mechanism for making it real. Doing
it is a two-part process.

The first part is setting your intention and deciding what you will
pay attention to in order to accomplish that intention. Your intention
is a reflection of your values. Dig down and ask yourself these two key
questions:

1. Why am I doing what I'm doing?

2. What goal or purpose will my involvement in this action
   serve?

The answers to these and similar questions will lead you to your
purpose. Ironically, this inquiry is likely to cause you to stop doing
some things because you will see that the activity, whatever it is, simply
isn't worth the effort.

The film *What the Bleep Do We Know?!* presents a colorful description of what happens when a person forms a clear intention. Well-
known authorities on brain functioning, such as neuroscientist and
pharmacologist Candace Pert, teach that seeing isn't believing, but rather believing is seeing. By clarifying your intention, you begin to focus
on what you believe in. The result, especially with paying attention, will
be a profound increase in the purposeful direction of your life. That's
part one.

The second and equally important part is making a commitment to pay attention. I first heard
about this two-part formula when
attending a national conference
sponsored by the Institute of No-
etic Sciences (IONS). I took their
advice and applied the formula

———————○———————

I read and walked for miles at night
along the beach, writing bad blank
verse and searching endlessly for
someone wonderful who would step
out of the darkness and change my
life. It never crossed my mind that
that person could be me.

—Anna Quindlen

———————○———————

throughout the conference and found that it worked. I learned more and created better relationships. Paying attention is the part of the recipe that gets us to keep paying attention rather than mindlessly walking around in la-la land.

If you don't pay attention to what you have decided is most important and slip back into old habits, you are likely to find yourself worrying about some past event, planning dinner while strategizing for an upcoming meeting, or thinking about whatever else is on your mind. The problem is that you cannot address those other tasks well while you are in the midst of another activity, nor are you paying full attention to what is going on right in front of you. My challenge to you is: If what you are doing isn't worth your full attention, then don't do it! While that may not always be a solution for you, consider it—it might be possible more often than you think. You will be respecting yourself and everyone else when you make the choice to be fully in the moment, wherever that moment is.

Activity: *Getting Focused*
This is all about you and your 2% Project, so it's time for you to get focused. Give your best answers to completing the following statements. Use your 2% Journal, as needed.

My *intention* in initiating my 2% Project is to _____
_____
_____

In order to realize that intention, I will pay *attention* to

    1. _____

    2. _____

    3. _____

> There are always reasons for doing what you do, but people often fail to take the time to become conscious of those reasons. Becoming conscious is your purpose here because you are focused on living your life well. Therefore, take a few more minutes to answer the WIIFM question—again, What's in it for me? This question may actually focus your response on your intention; therefore, you might even want to answer it first and then write your intention. What are your anticipated benefits for engaging in this 2% Project? Answer the following question in your 2% Journal: What's in it for me (what are the benefits I anticipate from engaging in my 2% Project and what benefits do I expect to gain by the completion of the Project)?

My daughter, Julia, is a young woman with special needs. She is challenged with learning disabilities, which affect her ability to communicate and often cause her to get frustrated quickly. She teaches me about paying attention daily. If I pay patient attention to what she's telling me, I understand her story, she feels heard, and she's happier and more relaxed. We all want to be seen and to be understood. We can only give that gift to one another through paying attention.

In The Artist's Way, Julia Cameron writes that "the quality of life is in proportion, always to the capacity for delight. The capacity for delight is the gift of paying attention" (1992, 53). I love this phrase—what a positive motivating force! Consider developing a 2% Project that will expand the delight in your life as you pay increasing attention to what really matters. This is another way of saying you are expanding your awareness or your consciousness. If you aren't paying keen attention to the present moment, then you are missing the joy it offers. Instead, you are guaranteed to be reworking the past or projecting the future. Isn't it strange how we can be longing for life with such gusto but that we keep missing it with all that planning? Design your 2% Project to meet your unique longing for a particular experience and get started on it in this present moment.

Engage Your EQ: *Self-Regard*

Having a positive sense of oneself is central to a healthy personal psychology. Psychologists such as Fritz Perls, Carl Rogers, and Gordon Allport are among the many who put the skill of self-regard at the forefront of successful engagement with life. The Bar-On EQi® (described in Chapter 1) begins its list of 15 factors with this skill. The key to positive self-regard is understanding and accepting yourself. Authentic self-regard is far from indulging in an ego trip based on denial. Instead, it is accepting yourself fully—warts and honors. We all have some of both. This knowledge is found through conscious awareness while practicing strong reflective skills.

You *can* increase your self-regard. Some have fallen into a defeatist or cynical attitude saying something like, "I just am what I am so deal with it." Don't you believe it for a second! If a person is motivated to change—and that is a pivotal *if*—then change is available. However, it does require focused commitment and an effective behavioral strategy. That may be a purpose of your 2% Project. Even if you don't initially include this as an intended goal, enhanced self-regard is likely to result from your success with your project.

Self-regard may be thought of as self-esteem—thinking well of yourself. However, there are many nuances like self-confidence and self-respect, all of which may not show up to the same degree in all areas of your life. Is there a difference between how you talk about yourself to others and your self talk?

This can happen because of your sense of self-worth or possibly for cultural reasons. Your self-worth may be consistent in that what you tell others about yourself is authentically how you feel. However, many people experience a disconnect. For instance, relentless media may cause you to see yourself as heavy and unattractive because you don't have a pencil-thin waist or six-pack abdominal muscles. This can lead to negative self-talk where you label yourself as fat, fraudulent, phony, inadequate, dumb, or some other epithet.

Yet, despite this negative internal state, perhaps you follow the strategy employed by Shakespeare's Lady Macbeth, to "put on a face to meet the faces that you meet." This can help you externally.

People might hold you in high regard, follow your leadership, and listen to your advice because you sound like a competent authority. However, if you are sabotaging yourself with negative self-talk, the incongruence will take a big toll. Subconsciously, people usually pick up on that disconnect. Additionally, internal self-doubt is a strong contributor to high levels of stress, which brings its own fallout. If this is your challenge, a 2% Project directed at gaining internal and external congruence is likely to be quite helpful.

Research by Shinobu Kitayama and Yukiko Uchida reported in the *Journal of Experimental Social Psychology* in 2003 addresses the cultural difference of the expression of self-regard in the U.S. and Japan. They found that while the Japanese speak modestly of their achievements to others, they use positive self-talk to reinforce themselves internally. However, if the Japanese were placed in a situation of social detachment, which is the more prevalent norm in North America, they expressed a pattern more like the North Americans of positive self-regard expressed both internally and externally. This finding shows that cultural and personal conditions influence self-regard, and those factors should be considered when evaluating whether one's self-regard is strong and healthy or is a drag on one's success.

Jim Collins, author of *Good to Great*, presents striking research about CEOs of the most successful companies: the skills exhibited by these leaders are a combination of humility and professional will focused on the success of the company. Collins writes that these "leaders channel their ego needs away from themselves and into the larger goal of building a great company....their ambition is first and foremost for the institution, not themselves" (2001, 21). To do this takes self-confidence and highly tested self-regard.

As you evaluate and develop your own self-regard, notice how much of your thinking centers on making yourself as important as possible. How much is focused on a higher purpose, such as your organization, community, family, or religious or spiritual beliefs? Collins' research is a powerful guide to the benefits of moving beyond personal ego. He emphasizes that his work reflects an empirical, not an ideological, finding, but it certainly documents our more idealistic beliefs about the value of dedicating ourselves to a higher good.

Activity: *Improving Self-Reflection*

Fortunately, there are many ways you can improve your skills in self-regard. Pay attention as you are implementing your 2% action plan, especially with your reflecting time, to notice how you feel and give yourself positive and realistic messages.

Some specific tactics you might employ are:

- Work with a resource such as *Feeling Good: The New Mood Therapy* (1980) by David Burns to improve your self-regard. This book, as well as many other books on this topic, rely on work by Robert Ellis to use cognitive skills to increase your self-regard. In essence, the process is if you have a debilitating thought, notice it, then challenge it with more accurate thinking. You can train yourself to think differently.

- To notice how you are feeling, you must first begin with making it okay to feel and to understand your feelings. Use the phrase "I feel _____ because _____." On a piece of paper, fill in this phrase five times a day for three weeks. You will be retraining your brain and creating a new habit.

- Use your reflection time to help you notice how you feel, what messages you give yourself (your intrinsic self-talk), and what messages you give others about how you feel about yourself. Notice whether those messages will support you in being fully alive to your possibilities.

BEING REFLECTIVE RATHER THAN *REFLEXIVE*

Along with the opposable thumb, reflective self-awareness is a distinguishing capacity of human beings. The bad news is that we use this capability so little; the good news is we can develop this skill.

I am passionate about the value of reflection, so I will use every incentive I can find to encourage you to develop and use your self-reflective skills. This capacity is at the heart of living an aware and intentional life. It is the crux of a life well lived and lived on purpose. Confucius is frequently quoted as saying that we can learn wisdom by three methods: "First, by reflection, which is noblest; second, by imitation, which is easiest; and third by experience, which is the bitterest." The 2% Solution is all about conscious personal development and requires persistent personal self-reflection to maximize success.

Understanding *reflective awareness* might best begin with a look at the current knowledge of brain functioning, as the terms *consciousness, awareness,* and *being reflective* are often used interchangeably. I looked in vain for precise and universally accepted definitions of these terms. The Scientific American Library's book entitled *Consciousness* by Allan Hobson seemed like a good place for guidance. He describes the development of consciousness from infancy with awareness of sensation and progressing to making "representations of representations" and finally to the adult level of being "aware of our awareness." He elaborates that the process is "the gradual building up of symbol upon symbol as brain circuit is added to brain circuit" (2000, 97).

> It is not so much the example of others we imitate as the reflection of ourselves in their eyes and the echo of ourselves in their worlds.
>
> —Eric Hoffer

Here's what is important to your life's 2% Solution: You are an adult, you have worked hard, and your brain has added brain circuit on brain circuit. Now it's time to engage the advanced course. Be aware of your awareness. Ask "Who Am I?" Understand what you do and why. This will lead you to clarity and the ability to engage your sense of humor about life. Use your 2% Project to grow this power.

BENEFITS OF SELF-REFLECTION

Engaging in self-reflection is an art form. And just as some prefer classical art, others cubist or impressionist, you need to make your individual choices regarding the kind of reflective process that serves you best. Recall the benefits of reflecting and then learn from a master reflector.

We are back to the WIIFM test. What benefits will you gain if you begin or increase your reflecting? Here are a few possibilities:

- Improved focus and clarity regarding what is important

- The opportunity to anticipate the consequences of your choices

- The ability to connect with deeper meaning in your life as you become more aware

- Improved morale

- Improved motivation as you become more aware of how to bring what is important to you to fruition

- Improved interpersonal relationships as you better understand the effects of your decisions

- Expanded ability to maintain deeper connections which otherwise get lost in e-mail and the computerized, digital world

- Enhanced ability to create a natural path for acting ethically because you are telling the truth

- Focused healing, which springs from reduced stress brought on by making choices that align with your life

A subtle and very important benefit can be the way that being aware causes natural ethical behavior. In the Introduction and in Chapter 2, the Fab Four benefits of living in accord with a 2% Solution were discussed. The second of these is congruency: When you align your values with your daily living, there is true internal accountability, which creates authentic integrity that arises out of deep and honest personal reflection. It doesn't have to take a lot of time, but it does have to be honest.

REFLECTING IS NOT A SPECTATOR SPORT

A commitment to reflecting conjures up images of monks in endless days of silence. Hours of sitting. Untenable yoga positions. A barren landscape. A paucity of chocolate. However, reflecting is not a period of endless watching and waiting. Although it's often done quietly, it's also done actively.

Some of us are so accustomed to barreling forward at top speed that the idea of putting aside our lists, shutting down e-mail, and turning off our cell phones is downright intimidating. Not to worry—you don't have to live a monastic life to do some mind blowing, heart stop-

> Knowing others is wisdom, knowing yourself is enlightenment.
>
> —Lao Tzu

ping, soul searching. Like Sam and his friend in the classic Dr. Seuss book, *Green Eggs and Ham*, you can do it in the rain, on a train, on a boat, with a goat, here, there, or anywhere! A few possibilities include:

1. **Pen and paper.** Keep a journal, create fictional characters that have a dialogue, or write letters to yourself or to a friend or colleague.

2. **Shake, rattle, and roll.** Take the dog for a walk, hop on a bicycle, get out your knitting needles, turn on the music, clean the house, work in the garden, bake some bread, or do whatever it is that helps you relax, think, and explore inside yourself.

3. **Java jaunt.** Go have coffee with a friend and have an intimate conversation; start a group whose purpose is to gather and reflect; join a support group; if appropriate, participate in the many forms of 12-Step groups, such as AA; or join a leadership development group where people take time to listen to one another. I belong to a group that named itself in honor of the outcome it seeks—the Wisdom Community. Our anchor behavior is reflecting; we go around the circle as soon as we get together, listening with the ears of our hearts to one another. We wouldn't trade

our community and its joys for anything! E-mail allows us to keep the reflecting going even when we aren't together.

Take the questionnaire which follows to clarify the best reflecting styles for you. Use your 2% Journal, as needed.

Activity: *Identify Your Style*

I can look honestly into the interior of my life when I reflect by
_____. To answer
this question, fill out the following form.

Instructions: Place a number from 1 to 10 in the blank by each of these categories. 10 is the highest, indicating a highly preferred way. Rate each one independently; thus, all may have the same or different numbers.

_____ I like to be alone and quiet when I observe important parts of my life.

_____ I like to be with friends who truly listen and give insightful follow up when I observe and reflect on what's happening in important aspects of my life.

_____ I like to be with professional peers, who truly listen, will challenge me, and give insightful follow up when I observe and reflect on what's happening in important moments of my life.

Instructions: Check the ones most supportive for you.
I am more likely to be reflective (to think things through with honesty and compassionate rigor) when I:

_____ write
_____ talk
_____ am with other people
_____ am alone
_____ am with a few select people

_____ am in a structured group with a facilitator
_____ am in an unstructured environment with people I know well

Instructions: Now pull it all together using all the categories you have checked (including the scores from the first three items) by finishing this sentence:

I am most likely to reflect with honesty and compassionate rigor when

_____

_____

_____

UPDATING YOUR 2% ACTION PLAN

Now you're ready to act on your insightfulness. Your form for tracking your 2% Project, the 2% Action Plan, follows. It is a bit different from the version in Chapter 2 as I have added a sixth step that asks you to list how you will reflect as you implement your project. This is an essential step. It's the path to your "ah ha's." Pursue your reflecting path at least once a week to quietly do an overview of your project and how it is influencing your life. Additionally, the support team you identify in step 4 is likely to be a good source of meaningful mirroring, or reflecting, from others.

If you weren't ready to fill this form in when reading Chapter 2, now might be a great time. If you did fill it in, add the new step 6.

My 2% Action Plan

1. My 2% Project is:

2. I recognize that specific action is important, so I will set specific times for my project (list the day and hour when you'll work on your 2% Project and what you'll do):

Day	Time	Action
Monday		
Tuesday		
Wednesday		
Thursday		
Friday		
Saturday		
Sunday		

Or you might want a weekly format:

Week 1   I will (fill in the dates and actions for the first week):

Week 2   I will (continue this throughout your project):

3. Tools or other support items I need are:

4. My support team (name the people who will support you in accomplishing your goals, people who know you well enough to give you meaningful and considerate feedback):

5. My goals:

   • My goals for the first month are:

   • My goals for the first six months are:

6. I will regularly reflect on my success by:

7. How I will know that I'm on track to implementing my 2% Project:

2% in Motion

RECOVERY, ONE DAY AT A TIME

Raul's life was about to implode, leading him to lose everything, when he finally admitted he had a problem with alcohol and joined AA. He had a comfortable lifestyle and enjoyed a great social life, but he was dangerously close to losing it all because of an alcohol addiction that was consuming him. He was terrified by the thought of admitting his alcoholism. He was scared witless about the prospect of not doing something about it. Truthful self-reflection led him to define his 2% Project as "taking better care of Raul." It has been a difficult but life-saving 2% effort for Raul. He committed to journaling for 30 minutes a day after meetings so he could honestly reflect on what he heard. His personal commitment was to be honest with compassion.

A lot of thought and awareness has gone into this deep caring he gives himself. Several years into the process, Raul is committed to always living with a 2% Project so that his potential to be a whole person doesn't go unrealized. He knows his personal development is an ongoing, lifelong process. Raul happily recounts that his hard work "continues to unfold much beauty and richness in my life—one that has given me the mental, physical, spiritual health that my heart and soul yearned for all my life."

Raul's 2% Project helped him go into recovery, one day at a time. Along the way, he also found that he was so focused on his professional success that it was hurting his relationship with his significant other and his family. As his personal transformation unfolded, Raul lost his partner, grew dynamically in his career, gained sobriety, and eventually found a new partner. It has been a long and often painful journey with many ups and downs, but Raul never equivocates about the huge value his focused motivation has brought him. Now he pays close attention to living his life to the fullest in a way that gives credence and attention to all that he loves. %

THE CORE OF THE 12-STEP PROCESS

The 12-Step process is difficult and life saving. Addictions, such as to alcohol and drugs, are as challenging as any problem can be. The success rate in beating them is far too low, as I know all too well. My dear brother, Bob, succumbed to the disease a year ago, finally committing suicide when career, marriage, and family fell apart.

I have other family members successfully working the AA program, and I find it hard to fully express my gratitude for this. For a time, I participated in Adult Children of Alcoholics and found the 12 steps to require honesty at the deepest level. Fortunately, it is a challenge followed by a deep blessing for those who partake of its wisdom. Two of the steps are based on a reflection process that is as thorough as you can find. Step 4 calls for making "a searching and fearless moral inventory of ourselves," and step 5 reads that we "admitted to God, to ourselves and to another human being the exact nature of our wrongs." People who go through and stick to the 12-Step program don't need a federal law to make them honest; they live it every day in their meetings and in their personal work. I honor all the beautiful people who acknowledge this struggle and work hard. Their healing affects them and at least millions of others on the planet.

While most of us are blessed with not having to struggle with addictions at the level folks in AA and NA (Narcotics Anonymous) do, we all have challenges and incredible temptations in our consumer-oriented society. Embracing regular reflective practices helps us resist the messages of the constant advertising and instead follow our heart's desire. Design your 2% Solution to help guide you down this road.

TUNE IN YOUR MIND

- Articulate your sense of self by answering the question "Who am I?" This facilitates your level of full engagement in your life.

- Focus on your 2% Project to take advantage of the possibilities of better understanding yourself.

- Your understanding of your true identity comes through expanding your emotional intelligence skills with self-regard.

- Being aware that we are aware means living a conscious life. It is the key to living your life on purpose. Reflecting is one of your best strategies to enhance this skill. Use your preferred reflective style to reflect regularly and add it to your 2% Project implementation plan.

- Take advantage of the links between accountability, emotional intelligence, and your 2% Solution to live your life in a naturally ethical way.

TUNE OUT THE NOISE

- Don't numb out. Rather, notice what is happening in your life so you can take charge.

- Avoid emotionally skating when talking with trusted peers or companions. Receiving their reflective feedback will help you tell the truth.

A SNEAK PREVIEW

Ever wonder just how to really maximize your possibilities and still live a balanced life? Does it seem like an either/or proposition? Learn how you can have it both ways and be happy. You learned to worry—research shows that you can learn to be happy. Think positively!

5/

PURSUE "PASSIONATE EQUILIBRIUM"

Simplicity as a Solution

*P*aul and Tina were living the high life. They had great jobs, earned salaries that went a long way, and were respected and well-liked by their colleagues. In short, they were the consummate career couple.

Tina completed her Ph.D. with honors and had a very stimulating and satisfying position working closely with the dean at a well-known medical school. Life should have been perfect. It wasn't. Tina longed for a child. Paul did not—not at all.

This single discrepancy could not accommodate compromise, only consensus, and Tina and Paul couldn't reconcile the question. Finally, they divorced, and to their credit, did it amicably. Tina then summoned all her courage and took the biggest chance of her life so far—she adopted a child as a single parent. She is now the proud parent of Mary, who has made all the difference in Tina's life. Of course, Tina is making all the difference in Mary's life too! The remarkable part is that even though Tina complicated her life greatly and added infinite responsibility, she is even more successful as the new assistant dean. %

Imagine how many different ways you *could* live your life. You could run your own little boutique business or oversee a cast of thousands. Perhaps you want to dance all night and bake all day. Maybe you want to travel the globe and have a small farm. Stay home and raise a family but still taste-test chocolates for Godiva. Maybe you want to be a CEO *and* a soccer parent.

Sometimes life imitates art, but often it feels like a treadmill, moving all the time but going nowhere with the same old view. Work. Chores. Errands. Bills. Do it all over tomorrow.

Other times, it's just a rat race. The physicists didn't really need to prove that the pace of life is accelerating—most people are barely hanging on. When the focus is just trying to hang on, though, it's pretty tough to truly engage in the full experience. The stress overwhelms the joy, the dissatisfaction squelches the passion, and the pace precludes renewal.

Living with zest and getting some rest—are both possible? Yes, and it's always about balance. A new PDA with more horsepower won't get you there. A hands-free cell phone or a wireless Internet connection won't do it either. You'll be able to multiply your multitasking, but all the gadgets in the world won't serve up passionate equilibrium. Passionate equilibrium is what *will* get you there.

Passionate equilibrium is about how you live your life. With it, you can claim the delicate balance of truly bringing your best gifts to life while also living in a healthy, sane fashion. You'll be able to do what you love and actually love it while you're doing it, because you'll slow down long enough to enjoy it all.

Explore passionate equilibrium and make it a vital part of your life when you:

- Identify your true passion and practice saying *no* to the surrounding noise that leads to chaotic diversions rather than a balanced and meaningful life.

- Break through resistance and reluctance to claim success.

- Address gaps in job and life satisfaction by learning how to expand your EQ skills and be happy.

- Check in with your 2% Project to be sure you're on track to combine passion, patience, and practice.

JUST SAY *YES*!

Do you sometimes dream about what you would do with your life *if only...*? If only you had the energy. The money. The opportunity for the right training or education. Excuses are a dime a dozen and obstacles are around every corner. There are always a million reasons why something can't be done, but it just takes one reason to do it—and you can find that reason in your Esprit d'Core!

Think for a minute of a time when you were fully enthusiastic, meeting life with zest, overflowing with gung-ho, go-for-it behavior. Was it fun? Was it contagious to others? Do you look back at the time fondly? Make a few notes about how you got there and how to get back there in the future.

What keeps you from living that way all the time? You may think it is just too hard to live a life filled with zest. The choices aren't as narrow as living with passion at a pace faster than the speed of light or living a simple, uncomplicated life that offers balance and rest at the expense of passion. The strategy calls for the appropriate doses of correct thinking, action, and balance. Of course, life sometimes deals some hard blows, but that need not stop you from finding a way to express your passion.

SITTING TALL

My brother Ken is challenged with severe multiple sclerosis, or MS. His whole life happens from a chair, but he's no spectator. He doesn't own a car because he can't drive, so he has to rely upon his wheelchair, public transportation, family, and friends to get around town. Even still, this doesn't slow him down.

Life is neither simple nor easy for Ken, yet he has found many ways to pursue his passions and bring his gifts to the world. When he had more mobility, he was co-leader of a Boy Scout troop for physically challenged boys. Later, he served on the board for his housing association. Although his health has continued to decline, he hasn't quit. He approaches every day with cheerfulness and gratitude, happy to be a part of life. Ken is passionate about his independence. He works fiercely to take care of himself, and he does it with more courage and grace than you can imagine. He is a role model for so many, including myself. I am awed and inspired by him, and when I am with him, I am humbled by how pale my own challenges are. I want to be a better human being because of him. What a gift he is to all who know him!

A DEFINING MOMENT

Is it safe to bring your passion, your zest, fully alive? If something says it's not, befriend that voice and investigate to find what changes it needs to help you go for it.

Some people may feel that it's too risky to bring their passion fully alive. They may worry that it will consume them or force them to abandon their loved ones or other joys. Understandably, most people don't want to give up most of their life to develop one gift. This is even truer for the many who feel a hunger to live simply. Of course there is always some give and take, but you can bring your best to your life, you can engage in your passion, and also live a balanced life. Neither value will be accomplished to the extreme; there will be a balance. Yet by giving time and expression to both, you are likely to feel more fulfilled and less harassed.

The bottom line for building this discipline requires that you express clarity about your values through all your important choices. It means that once you make a decision, you actively pursue it.

DO IT ON YOUR OWN TERMS

Grace and Grit (1991) is in my top 10 favorite books of all time. The always loving and sometimes painful story covers the five years of Ken and Treya Wilber's marriage during which they struggled with Treya's breast cancer. The authors invite the reader into the heart of their anguishing and uplifting love story. Their story includes the journal writing Treya did during the time, interspersed with Ken's thoughts and recounting of his experience. Treya was in her 30s and had been an activist in many causes. Ken Wilber was becoming one of the world's greatest living philosophers.

Treya wrote of her effort to balance being and doing. As it became increasingly apparent that she might not live long, Treya faced a powerful struggle, feeling despondent that she hadn't had enough time to bring her gift to the world. "Yes, I have contributed," she wrote, "but not enough." No amount of assurance from Ken or others about her value helped her feel sufficient about her contributions during her life.

Treya's illness brought her to her knees at times, but it also raised her to what I can only call "divine wisdom." Ken writes that her archetypal issue was "being versus doing, allowing versus controlling, trusting versus defending" (166). We all have archetypal issues; perhaps meeting the challenge they present us is the reason we are on this planet. Dealing with our core life challenges is usually at the heart of our life's deepest purpose. If we are not facing those challenges, we will begin to swing out of balance and struggle with denial.

When Treya found the answer to her personal quandary, she described it as a marriage of the "Carmelites' [Catholic nuns] emphasis on passion with the Buddhists' parallel emphasis on equanimity" (338). Her writing seems to sing the phrase of passionate equanimity over and over. Finally she found the answer to her struggle! She describes her phrase as "to be fully passionate about all aspects of life, about one's relationship with spirit, to care to the depths of one's being but with no trace of clinging or holding." Treya continues, "The first part of my life was learning passion. The life after cancer, equanimity" (338–39). This was her balance of being and doing.

When I read this phrase I felt a surge of excitement. Yes! I recognized the struggle. How much should I do? I have many gifts to give, but surely it isn't valuable to live my life in an exhausted state. There's a phrase some revolutionaries use that they find inspirational: "We sleep when we die." That doesn't feel authentic or wise to me; I need passion with balance.

Equanimity implies composure; Webster's defines it as "evenness of mental disposition." *Equilibrium* is defined as a "state of balance between or among opposing forces or processes. . . . a state of intellectual or emotional balance." So for me the guiding phrase is similar to Treya's, but different. My watchword is *passionate equilibrium!*

My excitement bubbled over; I couldn't wait until the women's leadership group I was in met again and I could tell them *The Answer*. Part of my passion to share the concept and process of the 2% Solution with the world comes from the tremendous lift I received once I could finally articulate my life's inner goal—to live with passionate equilibrium. While I believe strongly that all of us will benefit from both passionate engagement and balance in our lives, I also know that *you* will only be able to articulate what is most important to you through connecting with your core challenge. What phrase best represents your challenge?

You can't force your way to authentic discovery—it requires a balance of zest and rest, a harmony between passion and equilibrium. Claiming this balance is what yields a graceful life. A Buddhist practice that can help with this is to come to a full stop when things are starting to get too hectic and assume the mind set of "nowhere to go, nothing to do."

Passionate equilibrium is a real-world game plan. It's not pie-in-the-sky perfectionism; rather it is a continual learning process. As you commit to nurture all of yourself, rest and zest both happen, each in its own season and rhythm, but not always according to your schedule. So you need to learn to balance your expectations as well.

....
JUST SAY *NO*!

My book agent, Michael, is unique and insightful. One early day in the life of this book, he mentioned the importance of cutting out the noise in our lives. "That," he said, "is a critical benefit of the 2% Solution." He is a good role model. Amazingly, he cuts out the noise in his life by not receiving e-mail. It's mind-boggling to me that a busy professional with commitments and engagements across the world can pull off something that drastic in the 21st century! Michael demonstrates the possibility of gaining freedom by not surrendering to others' expectations.

Noise can be too many social events with neighbors, cell phone calls, season tickets that you don't enjoy, overscheduled kids, and anything else that feels burdensome on a routine basis. Noise is the stuff that is hard on your lifestyle, but for some reason you believe you have to tolerate it. You don't—at least not always. Ask Michael. Few of us would think we could run work successfully without e-mail, yet perhaps we could. Check out the noise in your life by working with this questionnaire.

Activity: *Turning Down the Volume*

1. Make a list of all your complaints for a few days. What is irritating, annoying, painful, or just makes things seem jumpy and out of alignment?

2. After you have gathered some data, sit quietly. First enjoy some relaxing, meditative time. Then begin to imagine what a more peaceful life would look and sound like. Feel the experience of a quieter atmosphere in your life. List some concrete examples of how things would sound, feel, and look.

3. Ask yourself what is different. What could change that would bring this marvelous peace?

4. Make the change if you're ready.

Most of us live in an environment that is truly noisy. It may be traffic, sirens, kids, or machinery. In a way it doesn't matter where the noise comes from; no matter the source, it has a stressful effect. That makes it even more important for you to choose to eliminate distractions that don't provide sufficient benefit to justify their cost. Are you ready?

2% in Motion

GETTING A LIFE

Dona left a vice president position in marketing with a large telecommunications firm to earn a Ph.D. in literature as a part of her 2% Solution. She also worked on expanding her self-esteem. Dona explained that "every time something big happened to me—accolades, and awards and so on, I would brush it off and instead continue to agonize over something I didn't do. I was constantly devaluing my own accomplishments." She created a 2% Solution to be more willing to trust and be less critical of herself. Her 2% Project led her to a life coach, to school, and to give up the world of high tech. Her goal was to trust that others would accept and appreciate her for who she was, as her authentic self.

Today she is measuring her success by her ability to appreciate and celebrate herself when great things happen—like when she has an article accepted in a juried professional journal. Interestingly, she discovered that, "The major shift is in what I value in life." Dona doesn't regret leaving the high tech world and loves being an adjunct professor at a private university. She is also giving up her penchant toward perfectionism by taking a jewelry making class, where she knows she will have fun but not be great.

Dona has some advice for everyone moving along the 2% path. She says that vision is the most important part of choosing your 2% Solution. It should be more about where and who you want to be, not fixing what is wrong with you. I couldn't agree with Dona more. The guidance you received in Chapter 3 to build on your strengths works when you combine your vision and strengths with action. 🅐

YOU CAN JUGGLE, BUT CAN YOU BALANCE?

Nearly every adult I know is juggling lots of competing priorities, but not many are as good at balancing their lives as they are at juggling tasks.

Passion and balance are two distinct values, and they work best when brought together. The goal is to learn how to have both in the proper proportion. First, explore each value individually and see how it plays out in your life. We will begin with simplicity and balance.

Living a balanced life implies that you give time to many important dimensions of your life. Family, community, professional development, and religious or spiritual development are often named as the most critical components—all requiring meaningful attention. If you become so engaged with one or two components that the other dimensions are neglected, you'll eventually feel disconnected from your Esprit d'Core and your life won't feel harmonious.

A balanced lifestyle and the value of simplicity have to go together, or you are likely to experience more pain than gain as you realign your priorities. Suppose you decide you just can't live without playing music, so you schedule seven hours a week for practice, and you also decide that you can no longer live without meditating, so you add in five hours for this activity. Now you are twelve hours busier. Have you complicated or simplified your life? In adding in these other two goals, did you give up anything else? If you were already sleepwalking because you were too busy, you may have made your life miserable in the attempt to make it better.

This unsustainable change is doomed to fail, and it very well might leave you with the tragic misconception that becoming your true self is just impossible. That's not true! Whatever way you approach living your life, you need to pay attention to both balance *and* simplicity. Balance allows you to give time to all the critical segments of your life, and simplicity keeps your own expectations manageable. Add passion to this mix and you have the formula for a life lived to its fullest.

Now let's look at how to bring that desire for making music and meditating realistically into your life. First, examine your current schedule honestly to see what you can give up that isn't as rewarding. Remember, some people live great lives without spending an hour or two writing e-mails each evening so don't assume you have to maintain the same level of noise. Next evaluate how much time you really need for the music and meditation—can you adjust the initial quantity of time? The final question is whether it is a good choice to add both to your life right now.

. . . .

'TIS A GIFT TO BE SIMPLE

Do you often talk about needing more simplicity in your life? Do a quick personal check: On a scale of 1 to 10, with 10 being highest, how important is simplicity to you? And how do you define it?

Richard Gregg is credited with coining the term *voluntary simplicity*, which he discussed in his 1936 book *The Value of Voluntary Simplicity*. Imagine how complex our lives have become in the time since he started asking us to be conscious about our lifestyle! And the idea is gaining ground: my Google search listed over *forty-five million* entries on simplicity! (I was tickled to discover that the first entry was for Simplicity sewing patterns, which I used in my 4-H Club while growing up.)

Probably the biggest challenge to living simply is the extreme preoccupation with materialism that dominates much of society and permeates our personal lives. John de Graaf, David Wann, and Thomas H. Naylor addressed this in their book, *Affluenza: The All-Consuming Epidemic* (2002), which aptly names our sickness. They explore the personal, social, economic, and environmental costs of over-consumption in North America. A quick search on the Web or in any bookstore will lead you to many other titles on how to live simply.

Read as many of these as it takes for you to decide to live your life authentically. Making that choice will help immunize you to the media and pressures promoting over-consumption. But don't get busier reading *about* simplicity

> A little simplification would be the first step toward rational living, I think.
>
> —Eleanor Roosevelt

and balance; instead, begin to *live* it. Use your 2% Project to connect with your inner wisdom, align with your values, and make your choices consciously. Pay attention to blending zest and rest.

A big part of the challenge has to do with your relationship with *things*. How much stuff do you need and how big does your house or apartment have to be for you to feel okay, happy, successful, fulfilled?

Spend some time reflecting on how much of your life is run by your relationship to objects. If you have substantial debt and you are working to pay the interest, is that debt worth it? Most of us could have much more control over our finances than we realize. For many of us, our relationship with objects, and the constant search for more, makes us feel edgy and unfulfilled. What does a more balanced and simple lifestyle mean for you?

A DEFINING MOMENT

Notice whether your engagement with the world is what Martin Buber called an "I–thou," or sacred, relationship, or an "I–it" engagement, which is merely practical.

Activity: *A Simpler Life for Me*

- My answer to how much I want simplicity on a scale of 1 to 10 is _____.

- I define simplicity as _____
_____
_____
_____

- As I brainstorm, the following are possible places where I can make changes and allow my life to be less crazed:
_____
_____
_____

Some of the key aspects to address if you are conducting a balance/ simplicity inventory are how you relate with:

- Money

- Professional development

- Family

- Friends

- Community

- Religious or spiritual development
- Peace
- Rest
- Pleasurable or recreational activities
- Hobbies
- Integrated living—a whole life

Consider whether you are making the zest/rest trade off. Are you *doing* now so you can be peaceful later? Be sure you aren't deceiving yourself and allowing the path of doing to go on and on and on. . . Of course, be just as challenging with yourself as you review your rest phase. Which aspect most reflects your challenge? Are you designing your 2% Project to help you respond?

ATTAINING BALANCE THROUGH YOUR 2% PROJECT

As I interviewed people about their 2% Projects, I asked how much their project contributed to better balancing their life. Some said not at al—their project turned their life upside down. For example, Mary, who focused on developing an authentic life and letting her creative side lead, said the resulting turmoil in her life when she first started reorienting her work focus was quite a challenge. Along the way she found a new balance, and she insists she wouldn't give up that deeply questioning time for anything. Now that she has been implementing her project for over five years, Mary has developed a new life with the opportunity to have a more authentic engagement with the right amount of zest and rest. Similarly, Tina, whose story begins this chapter, became a single mom while leading a challenging professional life. Even though her life became more complex, the changes caused her to become clearer about her priorities and what to keep in her life.

Terry, whose story is at the beginning of Chapter 4, is living more simply. She went through a period of substantial loss, which triggered her inquiry into who she really is. Part of Terry's answer is that she is a woman who can live simply. She no longer has a big corporate salary, and she recognizes that she does not need it. She's happy, relaxed, and wonderful to be with.

··

THE PASSIONATE PREROGATIVE

Beginning the journey of claiming your own happiness through balancing and simplifying your life takes conscious intention and attention. It develops through reflecting on and clarifying your priorities. The wisdom gained is a lifesaver when you are confronted with a vast number of choices. You can respond from your inner wisdom, which will guide you to choices that are fulfilling.

Living life with passion is a choice. Sometimes it will come very easily, while at other times it may be quite challenging. No matter what, it always requires that you pay attention to how you are living your life. As you engage in reflecting about your choices, you come to know what you are called to do. Identifying your passion is the biggest step of all, but there are other key steps, including clearing out the clutter in your life so you have the opportunity to fully engage with your passion.

Your 2% Solution can be your tool for allowing yourself to live passionately. One barrier to engaging with your passion can be a sense of being overwhelmed, that it will consume your life. However, if you take it slowly, engage in a small-scale operation, as the 2% Process calls for, you can safely experiment. It gives you a chance to play with your passion, to give it airtime without having to make a wholesale life change.

As you make space for what matters more, it is important that you remember the simplicity part of this prescription. It may seem paradoxical to start giving energy to something that excites you while simultaneously committing to simplicity. However, it is actually a way to live in harmony, in the genuine flow of life. If implementing your passion causes you problems with your health, relationships, or peace of mind, then something is wrong.

So, just what is passionate living? The best way to know is to view passionate engagement by some role models. Here are a few examples:

- A few minutes ago, my sister called to say her son, our beloved nephew, Alex is coming home from Iraq! He's been stationed there for nearly a year and there hasn't been a day our families have not worried about his safety. He has been deeply committed to doing his best, while maintaining his concern and compassion for his fellow soldiers as well as for the Iraqi people. Our family has been passionately committed to loving Alex and praying for him and all the people in Iraq—regardless of nationality. Passion comes in many forms.

• Diane Keaton won a Golden Globe award in 2004 for her role in *Something's Gotta Give*. She played her role with great passion, and her picture in *USA Today* portrayed pure delight. It seemed every cell of her being was celebrating. Keaton enjoyed pointing out that together she and her co-star Jack Nicholson were 125 years of age—love is not just for the young!

• Bethany Hamilton expresses her belief in life at a more profound level. At 13, while surfing in Hawaii she was attacked by a shark and lost her left arm. This young woman has gumption. She named her 1½ inch remaining arm stump "stumpie" and celebrated receiving a hybrid myoelectric arm prosthesis. The newspapers showed pictures of Bethany back in surfing competition just months after the accident. She defines zest.

• My friend Phil was the managing director of one of the biggest cities in the U.S. (with responsibilities similar to those of a city manager). He wrote to our leadership community and reflected on taking this new position. His e-mail described the first three days on the job, which included in one 24-hour period learning of a five-alarm fire in the middle of the night, a key employee dying unexpectedly the next morning, and dinner with the homeless that evening. He concluded his e-mail with this wisdom:

I will try to bring my heart, soul and mind to this job.
I will be challenged and will occasionally doubt myself from time to time as I have already done.
But I will be mindful of the sign I hung in my office today:

Faith is about going to the edge and then taking one more step. I have taken that one more step. May my faith be rekindled when the light loses its glow. May I have the courage to confront my fear. And may I have the strength to give of myself but hold steadfast to my ideals.

No one could say it better. So for each of us, the question is: Will I live my life fully; will I take that one more step? Will I do so with courage and the intent to hold steadfast to my ideals? If you want to live your life more fully, to give more profoundly, but don't know how, use your 2% Solution to guide you.

Activity: *Simplicity Value Statement*

Developing your Simplicity Value Statement is a way to make choices about the balance and simplicity in your life. Here's how:

1. Find the right stuff. Make a list of the key areas of your life. You can draw from the list in the last activity. Draw two large circles, and label the first one "Now" and the second one "Simpler Life," "Perfect Balance," or "My New Life." In the first circle, make a pie chart that shows how much time you give to each of the segments on your list. Some areas may not have any time associated with them right now and some may overlap. If you want to think it through more carefully, note that there are 168 hours in a week (7 days x 24 hours a day). Then approximate how many hours a week you put in critical areas. Begin by eliminating the hours used for sleeping, eating, interacting with family, and daily chores—those are nonnegotiable.

2. Take time to pause and reflect on what you've just developed. Let your heartfelt values come to you. What calls you? Visualize them happening, hear the sounds, feel the beauty and the power. Don't rush this valuable time spent reflecting.

3. Divide the pie. Fill in the second circle according to the balance and simplicity that you desire, knowing that it's in context of your current life conditions. If you have children at home or other life circumstances that call for your time, accept and value that part of your life. Peace of mind will make your life simpler. This is the equanimity Treya Wilber wrote about. It is part of creating a way to live with passionate equilibrium.

4. Leave your circles for a few days and let your new vision percolate. Spend some time just letting it resonate within you. Reflect and ponder.

5. Get into gear. Develop a written action plan based on your own personality style, spirituality, and your preferred ways of interacting with your world. Your action plan should be a very specific tactical plan that gets you from your current position to your vision.

6. Call a meeting. Have coffee or lunch with a close friend so you can share your plan with someone you trust. Choose a friend who will give you honest feedback, support you, and hold you accountable for the implementation of your plan.

7. Look in the mirror. Love yourself enough to hold yourself accountable.

8. Employ instant replay. Review your plan regularly to see whether you are on track. Don't go for the quick perusal; look at it in slow motion to really analyze the little details that lead to success and tweak your plan as needed. It is helpful to actually write down your

Pursue "Passionate Equilibrium" / 107

revisions so that the plan remains a living document that truly guides you.

9. Be honest with yourself about the values you are demonstrating through the choices you are making. Remember, change happens one decision at a time. If you discover that you don't like some of your choices, don't quit. Just recommit, revise as needed, and raise your awareness about your choices.

10. Get a supporting cast. Everyone needs a few good people on their team. Seek support or resources where you feel challenged. Celebrate your successes, your increased awareness, and your increasing peace of mind.

RESISTANCE AND RELUCTANCE

As you are moving toward increasing your own passionate equilibrium, notice any resistance you experience. Remember, at first just notice; don't resist the resistance. That would just tighten its hold. Whenever we move toward something new, we are likely to experience a countervailing desire to move back. Part of you says yes, part says no. For now, "maybe" is enough. This is part of the dance of change which we will explore in the next chapter.

> Until you are happy with whom you are you will never be happy with what you have.
>
> —Zig Ziglar

How does it feel to express your passion? Write about your feelings in your 2% Journal, take some notes, be curious. This, too, is a part of the unveiling of the 2% Solution in your life.

Engage Your EQ: *Happiness*

The U.S. Declaration of Independence is a remarkable document for many reasons, including this well-known phrase:

We hold these truths to be self-evident, that all men are created equal, that they are endowed by their Creator with certain unalienable Rights, that among these are Life, Liberty and the pursuit of Happiness.

How is it that in 1776 a small group of dedicated and rebellious souls so dramatically emphasized the value of happiness? One of the great commonalities among humans is the universal desire to be happy, and this core desire is one of the central motivators behind all major decisions we make.

Do you still doubt that you can increase your happiness through the application of your 2% Project? Fortunately, research and interest in this vital field is growing. Two excellent sources are Martin Seligman's book *Authentic Happiness* and the *Time Magazine* special edition on The Science of Happiness (January 17, 2005).

You really can grow your happiness. Scientists may debate the level of neurochemicals in the bloodstream and other details, but there is an overwhelming amount of evidence to indicate that you can choose behaviors to expand your happiness. In addition to all the research by world-renowned thinkers and institutions, just think back on all the 2% stories that reveal magnificent change; all of them have found strategies to grow their happiness.

According to some research, it does seem that we are born with a genetic set point—we have a predisposition for a certain amount of happiness. Genes influence such traits as having a sunny, easy-going personality; dealing well with stress; and feeling low levels of anxiety and depression. David Lykken studied this question working with 4,000 sets of twins, and he concluded "that about 50% of one's satisfaction with life comes from genetic programming" ("The New Science of Happiness," *Time*, January

17, 2005, A7). Even if Lykken is correct about the 50% factor, that still gives you 50% of your potential happiness to work with, and that's a lot!

An abundance of research shows that after a certain baseline of security is achieved, having more money or things doesn't make people happier. So how do you grow that 50% that is "nurtured?" In *Authentic Happiness*, Seligman identifies three types of happiness. The first level is associated with pleasure; it's the experience of hedonistic factors, such as chocolates or a new car. These are temporary and have only a minor effect on happiness. The second level, engagement, refers to the depth of our involvement, for example, with our work or community. The third, and most gratifying, is found when our action connects with meaning. This happens when we use our strengths and apply them to serve a larger purpose.

Notice these distinctions. If you truly want to build long-lasting happiness in your life, focus on using your personal strengths—what you are naturally good at—to make the world a better place. Be of service, contribute, and be grateful that you can do so. Other research finds that relationships are a vital factor in happiness, which is directly connected with being of service.

STRATEGIES FOR GROWING YOUR HAPPINESS

True happiness will resonate throughout your whole self—brain, body, heart, and soul. However, some strategies better serve one part than others. Seek a balance and have fun noticing the spillover benefits. Exercise is a classic example—of course it helps the body, but accordingly we can think more clearly, interact better, and connect with our sense of a higher power more clearly and enthusiastically.

- Regularly express gratitude—create a gratitude section in your 2% Journal.

- Relax and move, even for five minutes. Walk to a loved one and hug him or her; laugh while you're at it.

- Dance your way across the kitchen floor.

- Do your favorite exercise with your favorite music playing. (Yoga + rock and roll?? Oh well!)

- Watch funny movies or read the comics.

- Be kind—intentionally engage in five random acts of kindness a week.

- Applaud yourself. Pay attention to your thoughts. Every time you catch self-criticism, counter it with a positive appreciative message.

- Connect with people. Regularly hold a face-to-face conversation with someone you care about. E-mail a relative in the armed services, take your friend's children to a movie that is only for children, or visit someone isolated because of health constraints (pick up some flowers along the way).

- Be of service. Volunteer. Note that you are more likely to gain a sense of well-being if your service includes some one-on-one connection with the clients served by the organization, learning their names and hearing their stories. Being on the governing board is valuable but not the same.

---○---

You can gather some of the best data to support your happiness by paying attention to yourself. Notice when you feel happy and write it down. This form of deliberate reflective awareness will teach you

Three grand essentials to happiness in this life are something to do, something to love, and something to hope for.

—Joseph Addison

---○---

about you, and connecting that with action is what will make an actual difference in your life.

2% in Motion

BUSY AS THE LETTER B

Beaver. Bee. Bill. They all have one thing in common: They are high-achieving, busy, competent bundles of energy, but beavers and bees have nothing on Bill. He is one of the busiest men you can imagine. He is regional vice president of his national consulting firm; he is deeply involved with his three children, each with demanding schedules; and he is struggling with a difficult marriage. Yet Bill is working on his 2% Solution, asking questions, and praying for guidance to make wise choices. He writes in his journal, is in therapy, and reflects while he runs.

Bill first developed a 2% Project centered around getting greater clarity about telling the truth of coping with the stress at home. A deeply private person, he was concerned about talking about his marriage, yet stuffing it was getting increasingly depressing. He created a plan which led him to talking and reflecting about what was happening for 30 minutes a day. He found a few trusted friends and talked with them regularly, met with a therapist and gave himself quiet reflective time. %

Life is often difficult and extremely demanding—and that is often exactly when we need to intervene on our own behalf. If you're too busy to give your personal happiness 2% of your time, it's critical to ask yourself:

- What's really going on?

- Am I avoiding anything that seems too hard to deal with?

- Will the pain ever get better if I don't deal with this?

PERFORM WITH PASSION AND PRACTICE

Now, it's time to check in with your 2% Solution. Chapter 2 described the 10-Step Action Plan for implementing your 2% Project. It also included a form for creating a specific plan to help you commit 2% of your time to your project. Chapter 4 added another section to the plan—a place to note the results of your reflective time. Now that you have had a chance to learn and reflect since you first drew it up, this is a good time to check in again with your plan. Will it support an overall evolution for you, helping you enjoy both zest and rest? Is it likely to support your values?

No single 2% Project will lead to full self-actualization, but your project will be a meaningful step along the way. The right project will connect you with one of your passions. Working with it will be practice for expanding your full engagement with life. Don't expect too much of your first 2% Project—it may not move heaven and earth, but it should light a fire for you, and that is the stuff of progress!

TUNE IN YOUR MIND

- Identify your passion and say "no" to the surrounding noise that distracts you from your priorities.

- Learn to prioritize so that you can live simply with a balanced and fulfilling life.

- Live with an I–thou rather than an I–it relationship to your world.

- Clarify what happiness means to you.

- Be conscious of how satisfied you feel in the present moment so you can enjoy your happiness.

TUNE OUT THE NOISE

- Notice the consequences of surrendering to the materialistic impulses of our society. Don't get caught in living your life indebted because of objects.

- Know that you can live a fulfilled life. Don't settle for less.

A SNEAK PREVIEW

Chapter 6 supports you as you face that fierce and fiery dragon called change. It contains strategies that will give you the skills, tools, and confidence you need as you tackle the consequences of change and expand your EQ skill of flexibility.

6/

FACING CHANGE
Liberating Your Dragons

*C*arolyn was weary. She was a very successful sales manager with a major communications company, and that industry was a perpetual roller coaster. She took a sabbatical, and the time away gave her the space she needed to renew herself. She embarked on a 2% Project that inspired her to join a women's leadership group and engage in personal exploration. She did her share of journaling, thinking, and talking with other dynamic women in her leadership group, but it was a set of Russian matryoshka nesting dolls that captured her attention in a way she could never have imagined. The outer doll opened to reveal a slightly smaller doll, and that one did the same. Pretty soon there were seven of them, each smaller than the last.

Her original 2% Project was about speaking out loud, about showing the other facets of herself which she'd minimized in her job. Gradually, that minimization had given way to a separation from her core self that left her out of sorts. It was like the erosion of a boulder over time. It had happened so slowly that she didn't really notice it until there was a chronic undercurrent of dissatisfaction.

The nesting dolls provided a moment of insight so profound, it fundamentally altered Carolyn's 2% Project and her life. Looking at the dolls, it was suddenly clear that unless her 2% Project went all the *way to her innermost core, she wouldn't get the big payoff. The big payoff only happens when you make the big investment. That investment is not about quantity; it's all about quality. It means 100% of your energy and intentionality for 2% of your time. Carolyn realized this, and that meant summoning more courage.*

While speaking out loud was important, it did not reflect her Esprit d'Core. In truth, she wanted much more than to speak out loud; she wanted to speak in a very particular way. She wanted to be a minister. She went to theological school and is now actively engaged with her congregation.

Carolyn now proudly claims the title "Queen of the Squishy Stuff." She has become a minister and is happily living out her calling. Often it is a very demanding role, and she gets tired now and then, but her soul is never weary. %

Being alive is being able to grow; to be fully conscious is to choose the path of that growth. Change, an integral part of growth, can be a tumultuous process made difficult by both real and imagined obstacles. It is like trying to find your way out of a very complex maze. And if that isn't enough, we often invent false worries and what-ifs that paralyze us. The fears that stop us in our tracks are like dragons that leap out from behind a corner. They roar and pounce, shaking the very earth upon which we stand. They are so frightening we often can't face them, so we turn and bolt back to familiar ground. We sacrifice a dream to appease the beast, and our dream goes down in the fiery breath of an unwelcome guest.

There is no knight who will slay your dragons for you. It's a quest we each must take. However, one of the best ways to prepare for such an adventure is to hear the wisdom of those who have conquered their own dragons. As long as we have lived in communities, people have gathered to listen and to learn from those who have taken magical and perilous journeys. You can learn to face change through the inspired stories of those who turned their own 2% Solutions into routes to find meaning in a post-9/11 world, an event which has increased many people's commitment to live with purpose. With tools and practice, you can extinguish any dragon's fiery breath. In this chapter, you will learn how to:

- Understand your personal dragons.

- Channel the fire of fear into an authentic engagement with life.

- Respond to the evolutionary imperative and say *yes*.

- Pace the 2% Process to allow time to integrate shifts by expanding your EQ skill in flexibility.

MOAN AND GROAN—THEN GET MOVING!

If we could sit down together right now, we could tell each other of major challenges life has presented. We would literally moan as we tell our stories, and hopefully we would laugh some as well. Moaning and groaning can be useful—it helps release pent-up emotion and energy. The real question is whether you moan with a sense of humor and possibility, or with a sense of doom and victimization. Think about the difference behind these two attitudes.

To gain maximum freedom and maximize your potential, you must recognize the payoff and the payback to embracing change. If you determinedly embrace that you are *not* a victim of the world around you, you can reclaim the power you need to reach your cherished goal.

Your attitude dramatically affects your success as you respond to the inevitable changes in your life. Sometimes the most valuable attribute you can bring to change is to tell yourself, "Just deal with it!" If you're renting an apartment and your landlord puts the building up for sale, look for a new apartment. Moan and groan for an hour or a day if it will help, and then start packing. Of course, other times the change you are working with is more complex and takes lots of time and support.

CAN YOU SPARE A LITTLE CHANGE?

Change is a fact of life. In fact, people have known this since the dawn of time. Over three hundred years before the Common Era, Plato said, "Nothing endures but change." However, change still provokes consternation among most of us. Check out your perspective by completing this tiny but powerful equation: Change = _____.

If you want to hit a home run with your 2% Project, you need to know how you label and respond to change. Is it with ease, excitement, foreboding, or fading out? Your response to that short fill-in-the-blank statement gives you an indication about how your life works right now.

> Even if I knew that tomorrow the world would go to pieces, I would still plant my apple tree.
>
> —Martin Luther (1485–1546)

Remember the quote from Candace Pert that it is *not* that seeing is believing, but rather that believing is seeing? Perceptions create the threshold of your entire life. "Rather a bold assertion!" you may assert. I stand firm; It is a simple truth that we each create our own sense of reality. Here are a few basics to put a framework around change.

The only reliable elements in the physical world are:

- Whatever we know right now will change.

- Impermanence is the law of human and physical existence.

- Our attitudes and choices directly affect our resilience as we respond to change. If we are hopeful and optimistic, we are likely to begin looking for what good can come from a transition. If we are cynical and pessimistic, we will be looking for problems—and we will certainly find them.

- The more we resist change, the more difficulty we will experience. It is just like pulling on a knot instead of gently easing it open. Pull hard and you may never, ever get it open.

Happiness and optimism are my personal favorites among the 15 EQ skills. Time and again I witness the profound influence that optimism has on creating different experiences. Repeatedly, those who suffer from hopelessness have a completely different outcome than those who are optimistic, even though they find themselves in identical circumstances. That's why I keep circling back to the necessity of expanding your happiness and optimism. The difference in how you work with change when you bring your happiness and optimism to the table is like night and day. Remember, these components of emotional intelligence are skills. You *can* grow them!

··

LET YOUR HEART BREAK WIDE OPEN

According to most reports, approximately 160,000 people perished as a result of the giant tsunami that leapt out of the Indian Ocean on December 26, 2004. Our world will never be the same. The physical world changed when the tectonic plates shifted. You may be familiar with the theory called "Six Degrees of Separation." It holds that every person is connected to every other person in the world by no more than six people. So, somehow as author and reader, we are connected to the President of the United States, the Dalai Lama, the person who oversees how the hood ornament is installed on every Mercedes-Benz, a waiter in a Parisian café, a sherpa in the Himalayas, and on and on. It follows that we are all connected to the thousands and thousands who lost their lives in the tsunami—and to all the orphaned children who survived. We all have the same connection to those in New Orleans and nearby areas devastated by Hurricane Katrina.

Most of us have gone through hardships, some of which have been devastating for awhile. My ten-year-old niece was killed by a car when she was crossing the street to get the mail one day, and her father, my brother Bob, committed suicide two years later. One of my brothers has severe MS, and a close family member embezzled money from my company and from the companies of colleagues who will never speak to me again, even though we are active professionals in the same community. I know about pain and change. I also have experienced many delightful gifts in my life.

I am 56. That's long enough to have had many experiences. Fortunately, I was born with lots of optimism, and I intentionally expand the skill daily. Happiness has been a challenge I've had to work with diligently, and the work is not done. However, I'm happy to report I'm making progress!

While changes can feel overwhelming, I know that the feeling of being overwhelmed can be limited in time. For awhile we may feel swallowed by the pain, but eventually it is time to move forward, even if it is one minute at a time. When this kind of pain hits, seek help from professionals, colleagues, friends, or family. While the 2% Solution is about giving a voice to the core calling in your soul, it is *never* about suffering alone. Our world works best, and each of us heals and prospers the most, when we allow the strength of our interdependence to shine forth.

One of the spiritual teachers I have come to deeply appreciate over the years is a woman named Gangaji. Her style of teaching follows the Indian tradition of allowing members of her class (which can be over one hundred) to ask her whatever questions are troubling them. This is called *satsang*, which means "gathering in truth" in Sanskrit. I always come away from these meetings with more clarity about the beauty of surrendering to the truth. This was the message of her teacher Papaji, and his teacher, the renowned ascetic saint Ramana Maharshi.

One of my favorite points of wisdom I have heard Gangaji address is about responding authentically to grief. She advises that when loss hits, sit with it, fully feel the pain, and let your heart break wide open. You may have to come back to the grief repeatedly and sit with it again and again. When your heart breaks wide open, you transform—you change. Perhaps that is the point of life's journey.

Your 2% Solution will bring meaningful change to your life, and you will likely experience both resistance and welcoming of that change. Stay actively conscious and notice whether you are choosing to be an observer, or if you are totally engaged in the game, playing for all you are worth. Be curious about this transformative possibility. Part of change is usually experienced as conflict. Learn to be discerning: Say *yes* to the transformative parts of your change, but say *no* to unproductive conflict that just serves as a distraction. Use your wisdom and your powers of reflection and awareness to tell what is actually needed and what is just static or a diversion. This is certainly easier said than done, but it *is* possible. Life teaches us, and the 2% Process is a way to maximize those opportunities.

2% in Motion

EASING OFF CAN LEAD TO MORE

Melody describes herself as the quintessential Canadian. She has been evolving 2% Projects throughout her adult life, though she didn't know what to call them. At this time she describes her 2% Solution to be:

> *A whole-hearted and wholly hearted woman*
> *Who joyfully creates space and connects people*
> *For global learning and community action.*

Melody's 2% Project involved bringing Spiral Dynamics into Canada as a global learning endeavor. Her project aligned beautifully with her credo. Melody is a can-do bundle of energy, so she pulled off most of the trainings without a hitch. Then as she was working on one in Ottawa, she discovered that registrations for an upcoming training session were pitifully low. Not one to be easily disheartened, she used the 2% Process to support her intention. She figured that if 2% of the registrations she needed came in daily, she'd get enough to hold the training. This helped her frame the big project in a smaller, more doable way. It reduced her stress and expanded her flexibility, and now she looks back on her Ottawa experience as a day-by-day 2% Process. Melody sighed as she told me the story and said, "It helped me ease off." (I believe that is Canadian slang for "chill out.") %

BEYOND HERE MAY LAY DRAGONS

Dragons frequently represent frightful possibilities in the Western world. The metaphor "dragons in the closet" refers to scary things hidden away behind a closed door. Children are sometimes afraid of monsters in the closet, alligators under the bed, or things that go bump in the night. At the time when Columbus and others were searching for a new world, their maps would sometimes include the phrase "beyond here may lay dragons" to indicate the end of the known territory.

We understand our lives as they are now; even if they are messy or compromised, there is significant comfort in the familiarity. When you consider your 2% Solution and seriously think of inviting transformative change into your life, some part of you is likely to cry out, "Oh, no! Beyond here may lay dragons." Uncharted territories are scary, spooky, and may hold things that go bump in the night.

It's ultimately your choice: Do you want to open the door and face the dragon, or is the security and everything else you have—or don't have now—better? If you want to keep it closed, check out whether accommodating the limitation provides a false sense of security. What is the drag on your peace of mind because you are afraid that the dragon's fiery breath will burn a wide hole in that fragile door? Perhaps the real question is, "Are you willing to let your journey end at the dragon's door?" If you are ready to see what lies beyond the dragon, check to be sure you have the right support system to help you and then throw open the door with an air of collaboration.

REFRAMING DRAGONS

For the Chinese, dragons symbolize many good qualities, such as heroism, perseverance, nobility, and excellence. In the East, dragons are viewed more like angels than something to fear: Temples and shrines have been built to honor them. It seems that everything connected with Eastern dragons is blessed. The Year of the Dragon, which takes place every twelve years, is considered lucky. Asian astrologers assert that children born during Dragon Years enjoy health, wealth, and long life.

> I am king of paranoid in reverse. I suspect people of plotting to make me happy.
>
> —J. D. Salinger

The 2% Solution is a way to open the closet door, face your fears, and allow them to transform into valued teachers bringing health, wealth, and a long life. In truth, these benefits are probably much more reflective of our willingness, flexibility, and courageous engagement with life than they are limited by the year in which we are born. Face those fears and welcome freedom!

. . . .

TAKE THE TRUTH TEST

So screw your courage to the sticking point and start transforming your fear. Bringing your 2% Solution to life almost guarantees that you will encounter fear and resistance at different times and in different degrees. Naming fear is the first step to conquering it. Answer the following questionnaire in your 2% Journal to better understand the bogeymen you may face.

Activity: *Taking Inventory*

- When I quietly observe where my 2% Solution is taking me, I realize I'm concerned that:

  _____
  _____
  _____
  _____

- As I think about it, I realize that this is a concern to me because (think of this concern in both its best- and its worst-case scenarios):

  _____
  _____
  _____
  _____

Take 10 to 20 minutes and sit quietly with each possibility as if both the best- and worst-case scenarios happened. Then write about it. Here are some beginning sentences:

- I realize that if this happened, I would need to. . .
  Write about the support system available to you and
  the internal strengths you would draw on. Add reasons
  for both scenarios.

  _____

  _____

  _____

  _____

- I have been through other challenges and have come
  out fine, even great sometimes. These past survival
  stories help me remember that I can face this challenge
  as well. I will help myself remember this by (list some
  reminders):

  _____

  _____

  _____

  _____

- I will remember to give myself time to move through
  this process respectfully and to tap into the resources
  available to me. To accomplish this, I particularly want
  to remember:

  _____

  _____

  _____

  _____

PERCEPTION IS REALITY

Perception is tricky. Perception of any happening must, of necessity,
be a personal interpretation. Because it is the result of sensory data interacting with all that a person already knows, reality is created from
perceptions. This fact makes it very interesting to consider how often

you interpret events incorrectly. Truthfully, the answer could be always, because you never have all the data. Furthermore, your personal subjective experiences are not subject to any objective validation. How can you know if you're right? You have only your own experience of internal consistence over time and trust through which to judge what is real. While this level of theorizing could make the whole world seem just too ephemeral, there is a practical aspect to careful reality testing: We need to be mighty careful that we are solving the right problem.

> The only thing we have to fear is fear itself—nameless, unreasoning, unjustified, terror which paralyzes needed efforts to convert retreat into advance.
>
> —Franklin Delano Roosevelt, First Inaugural Address, March 4, 1933

What if your spouse or significant other comes home late three or four nights a week for a month? You may start getting worried that he or she is having an affair. You're ready for a confrontation, but, because it is Valentine's Day, you decide to wait until tomorrow. That night you are presented with a delightful wood carving which your spouse/partner made just for you. To do the work and surprise you required going to the neighbor's garage for an hour most nights for a month. Whew, you would be so glad you didn't do that confrontation, right?

This is the way of the world. We make interpretations, but we cannot be sure of their reality. So as you confront the process of change, be flexible enough to check out alternative interpretations. After making a thorough assessment of a matter, you must move forward. However, it is equally important to maintain willingness to shift your perception as you learn more and new light is cast on the situation.

While there are many definitions of perception in *Webster's Dictionary*, the one most relevant for us is that perception is: *Physical sensation as interpreted in the light of experience: the integration of sensory impressions of events in the external world by a conscious organism especially as a function of non-conscious expectations derived from past experience and serving as a basis for or as verified by further meaningful motivated action.*

Perception is also defined as "a direct or intuitive recognition." Apply this understanding to the concerns you just wrote about regarding your 2% Solution. Put yourself in the shoes of someone else who is fairly knowledgeable about your situation. Would he or she raise the same concerns? What different aspects would that person identify? What would be different about the plan of action?

Now you've gained at least one other perspective to consider. Ask others whom you respect for their reflections and opinions. We are interdependent beings; a different perspective is a strength and recognizing diverse perspectives is critical as part of our social and emotional competencies. They are the essence of reality testing.

Seek to understand your concerns from the big picture as well as zeroing in on the details. Zooming in and out changes perspective. A nice perk of changing your perspective by zooming out or expanding the frame is that you won't feel so hooked by your concerns. As you move into your analytical mind and play with different ways to understand the issues, the fire goes out of the dragon's breath. Dance with your concerns, seek to understand and face them, and you may find it is Puff the Magic Dragon from Peter, Paul, and Mary's song in your closet, not a fire-breathing monster!

THE MAP IS NOT THE TERRITORY

Neurolinguistic programming (NLP) is a way of working with and understanding human interactions based on understanding our neurology and linguistics. Richard Bandler and John Grinder founded the field based on their study of masters including Fritz Perls, Virginia Satir, Milton Erickson, and Gregory Bateson.

One of the key teachings of NLP is that the map is not the territory. Derived from the work of Alfred Korzybski, the father of general semantics, this phrase helps us remember that a good map will have similar structure to the land it seeks to represent, but it can never have all the details because it is always a representation, never reality. Similarly, we each create individual representations of our past and present experience, and these become the perceptual "maps" that guide the way we are living. Ideally, we do our best to update those maps, because failing to do so surely limits our success.

Ludwig von Bertalanffy, a prominent Austrian biologist, helps us understand that my thinking is not your thinking with his powerful statement that: "There are no facts flying around in nature as if they are butterflies that you put into a nice orderly collection. Our cognition is not a mirroring of ultimate reality but rather is an active process, in which we create models of the world. These models direct what we actually see, what we consider as fact" (Nichols and Schwartz, 1991, 105).

Freedom comes from accepting responsibility. Recognizing that we are personally responsible for the perceptions we have, and even more so for the attitude we have about our perceptions, is the key to gaining control in areas where it may otherwise seem impossible. Accepting responsibility for your attitude and the definition of reality you assert is among your most powerful strengths.

Activity: *Explore Your Map*

During our waking hours, our five senses constantly gather information about everything they detect going on in our world. Our brain/mind then assembles this data into perceptions of reality. Learn more about your role as a mapmaker and how you navigate in your life. Work in your 2% Journal with this questionnaire to explore how you have interpreted change in the past, and then consider whether your interpretations support you or sabotage your success.

1. Some of the most important changes in the workplace or my personal life that have impacted me over the last five years are:

2. When I think back on these changes, what concerns and hopes do I recognize about them?

3. How have they affected my work or personal life?

4. Given the fact that these changes have already taken place and my work and life experiences have changed, what are my hopes, needs, and goals regarding my future?

5. Is there baggage which it is time to let go of so that I can be free to move on? If so, what is it and how will I let go?

6. What will I have that I don't have now if I implement these changes to support me?

CHANNEL THE FIRE OF FEAR

"Fake it until you make it." I have heard many people advocate this game plan, including 12-Step groups and leadership development seminars, and I have used it often in my professional change work with individuals and groups. One of the best parts is people first laugh when I say it, but then it opens a window of possibility.

Take José. He and his colleague Anita constantly bickered and challenged each other. In fact, it was so intense that José was exhausted from it. He wanted to relate to Anita in a new way, but he was afraid of looking weak. He wanted a fresh start, but there were some complications.

Both were vying for management attention because they both wanted an upcoming promotion. Worse than that, José just felt incompetent. He didn't know how to get along with Anita. Finally, he decided to fake it. He decided that instead of talking with Anita about the issue, he would just change his behavior. He began paying attention to her feedback and learning along the way. He hit some bumps in the road, but he made progress. He took time to chat and learn more about her, complimented her accomplishments, and brought her coffee once in a while. Anita noticed and began to make changes herself. It's no fun to fight alone—it truly takes two to tango. José's management noticed as well, and his prospects for the promotion increased.

At first, José was afraid that he didn't have the skills to change a well-entrenched behavioral pattern. His willingness to face the fear and give change a chance made a big difference for him. The risk paid off: José learned the skills while gaining some peace of mind, and this positive experience will make it easier for him to take the next risk of facing his fears.

In *The Art of Happiness* (1998), the Dalai Lama explained to his co-author, Howard Cutler, his five-step process for overcoming obstacles. You will see a significant relationship between his five steps and what we are working with here. His five steps (220) are:

1. Learning

2. Conviction

3. Determination

4. Action

5. Effort

In the 2% Process we use reflection, through the 2% Journal and other methods of self-inquiry, for the learning stage. We use intention to cover the second and third steps of conviction and determination, and we implement 2% Projects to address action and effort. Good strategies usually have parallel steps. You can implement the Dalai Lama's approach to overcoming obstacles in your life through your 2% Project.

CHANGE IS AN ALLY!

What if you decide to view change as an ally? This goes back to perception, doesn't it? Why do we have such resistance with change? Because, simply put, it is hard. It's uncertain and it's often an ugly process. It can wreak havoc on your life. But the primary reason we generally dislike change is that it simultaneously leaves us in the throes of uncertainty while forcing us to activate the new connections in our brain that are essential to understanding and responding well to new situations.

Another reason is that change is often accompanied by conflict. Where would you place yourself on this continuum?

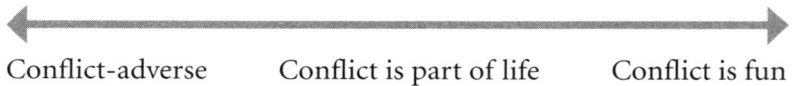

Conflict-adverse   Conflict is part of life   Conflict is fun

Either extreme can be too much. However, you are certain to miss opportunities if you are conflict-adverse. Some of the messiest situations I have facilitated were created by professionals who were very conflict-adverse. They tried to push all the conflict under the carpet, but that just doesn't work.

Other cultures view conflict far differently than the American culture does. For example, the Chinese character for conflict is made up of two different symbols superimposed: one indicates danger, the other opportunity. In the *I Ching*, a book of Chinese wisdom, conflict is seen as the state in which a person must be clear-headed, inwardly strong, and ready to come to terms by meeting the opponent halfway.

Changing your metaphors about conflict can help you accept the premise that conflict can be viewed as an opportunity—a time for growth or change. A positive metaphor is to view conflict as a dance that sways with the rhythm of the music. It may be smooth and flowing as in ballet, or a faster, jerkier movement as in a tap dance. We could view conflict as a tide that ebbs and flows smoothly and regularly, or more wildly as happens in stormy weather or at a bargaining table. Notice the metaphors used about conflict in your work environment. What supports appropriate conflict resolution in your life? What gets in the way?

Thomas Crum, an aikido master and educator, was a close friend and assistant to the singer John Denver. He wrote a classic book on conflict, *The Magic of Conflict* (1987), which I happily helped him promote. I recommend the book as a part of our conflict resolution work with clients. One time I had the privilege of spending a week learning aikido at a camp Crum offered in the Colorado mountains near Aspen. As I reached the point where I could toss a big man over my shoulder, I wondered why in the heck this art was coming so late in my life. Where was it when I really needed it, when I was growing up with five brothers, most of whom were engaged in football, wrestling, and tormenting my sister and me?

While many martial art forms focus on how to harm your opponent, aikido focuses on neutralizing any threat from a potential attacker, and it views the attempted violence as a misunderstanding that warrants education and correction, not punishment. Thus, Crum and other aikido masters consider how to neutralize their opponents instead of how to harm them.

TRANSITIONS AND LOSS

Resolving conflict successfully is always a process of transition. William Bridges, who wrote many works on this topic, one of the best of which is *Transitions* (1980), has identified three essential stages to the transition process: the ending, the neutral zone, and the beginning. People going through change often collapse or intermingle these stages in such confusion that none of them get completed well. When you are going through an important change, it is worth looking at each stage distinctly and determining where you are so that you can successfully complete any major transition and move forward with your life. The *ending* calls for a true recognition that something has stopped, that it is over with. Perhaps you have lost an important job, a loved one, or you are giving up a dream to be a senior manager by the time you are 40. When the recognition of the loss is finally accepted, it can be a shock. If others were impacted by the same change, they may have already accepted it and moved on. Thus, part of the challenge in working successfully through your change is to accept that each of us responds with our own timing.

The neutral zone occurs during the time when most of the work in accepting and responding to the change is happening internally. This can be extremely frustrating, as it may seem like you aren't getting anything done, that you just cannot seem to get on with it, or that other peers at the job site are not getting on with it. When you find yourself in this stage, you are likely to feel stuck. This can also be a time for experiencing some of the mourning related to the loss of something major from your life.

Some of the fear related to this process can come from the emotions related to mourning. Marilyn Ferguson, in *The Aquarian Conspiracy*, clarified what it is like with this metaphor: "it's Linus when his blanket is in the dryer. There is nothing to hold on to."

It is this fear that can cause people to cling to the mourning stage or to stay stuck in the neutral zone. It requires a careful balance to know how long to remain there. Ultimately, you have to trust your own internal wisdom to help guide you through this time.

A DEFINING MOMENT

The neutral zone is a powerful time. I call it being in "the creative void." This positive frame helps me know to value the process.

Bridges calls the final stage, oddly enough, the *beginning*. It is the time of excitement when people begin to understand the new dynamics of their transformed life, what it means to live without the loved one, or to be an effective and happy part of a new team. You get to choose a great deal of this because your *attitude* toward the workplace and toward yourself will greatly influence your ability to enjoy your job. Viktor Frankl recognized this when he was a prisoner in a Nazi concentration camp. He later became a universal source of inspiration when he wrote in *Man's Search for Meaning* (1959, 75), "The last of the human freedoms. . . [is] . . .to choose one's attitude in any given set of circumstances, to choose one's way."

THE FIVE STAGES OF LOSS

Elisabeth Kübler-Ross developed another way to understand how we adjust to the losses that occur with change. She identified the human grieving process as occurring in five stages. Her seminal work, beginning with her book *On Death and Dying* (1997), has helped many people make sense out of a confusing process. The five stages are denial, anger, bargaining, depression, and acceptance. When we are willing to recognize that transition always means the loss of something, it helps us be able and willing to go through the grieving process with improved acceptance.

What are your losses that affect your readiness to fully implement your 2% Solution? To picture the transition process, it is useful to merge Bridges' three stages of transition with Kübler-Ross' five stages of the grief process.

1. The ending process includes the stages of denial and anger.

2. The middle neutral process includes the stages of bargaining and depression, and may also incorporate resistance moving on to exploration, the precursor to acceptance.

3. The beginning process completes the transition with acceptance and perhaps commitment.

THE ELEPHANT IN THE ROOM

Now is a good time to check in with your 2% Project. How are you doing? Is your project well underway? Are you hiding from anything? By now, as you are probably digging in deeper to learn more about why your 2% calling is so important to

Hope sees the invisible, feels the intangible and achieves the impossible.

—Anonymous

you, you may be feeling a bit uncomfortable. If there is a scratchy element somewhere, take some time to notice it. Is there something that you need to notice even if it is uncomfortable?

There may be something going on that is so big, like an elephant standing in the middle of the room, that it's impossible *not* to notice it—but everyone ignores it as though it isn't there. Acknowledge the elephant if it's there. Talk about it; write about it. Don't let this big unnamed force generate negative energy in your life. Now is the time to claim your freedom!

Engage Your EQ: *Flexibility*

Cirque du Soleil's astonishing performances feature artists who move, spring, and dance in ways that are beyond imagination. It doesn't seem possible that humans could move with such fluidity and grace while accomplishing such amazing feats that seemingly defy physics. At times we need the same type of emotional flexibility. In today's multitasking world, we often need to be able to bend, stretch, and dance in place to meet our challenges. The EQ skill of flexibility shines most brightly in chaotic situations and can be a feat of near magical qualities.

Where is flexibility most important in your life? How does it relate to your 2% Solution? This skill is the essence of spontaneously adapting to change, which is one of the most valuable skills in the workplace and on the personal front as well.

Some might describe flexibility as being able to go with the flow. Rather than swimming upstream in a river or against the current in the ocean, a flexible person discerns the natural movement and uses it to accomplish his or her goals rather than resisting a force that is nearly certain to win.

You exercise your EQ skills in flexibility when you choose the right time to have a difficult conversation with a boss. You don't want to choose the day before year-end bonuses are given out, nor should you wait so long after a troubling event that the issue has become too stale to address. Using your skills in emotional flexibility requires sensitivity and balancing. Flexibility requires more than just "taking a chill pill," as our teenager would advise. It is usually not very helpful when people make remarks like, "Just calm down," "Just let it go," or, my favorite, "Just forget it."

Seldom can we truly "just" do any of this. Applying our skills in responding to change, surprise, and that which hits like a bolt from out of the blue takes adeptness and the ability to discriminate between multiple factors to craft the best response. The good news is that like any EQ competency, these skills can be enhanced, and keeping them in balance is itself an important part of your skill development.

Cheryl was excited about becoming the first Human Resources Director for a small city government. She had many capabilities and could easily see the big picture chock-full of opportunities. Cheryl genuinely liked people and aimed to please, but she quickly found herself inundated with requests that had been building up for years. She wanted to fulfill them all, but there was one big problem: Cheryl could not satisfy everyone—it was just too much. As we worked together, Cheryl discovered that while her skills in flexibility were an asset, the same skill became a liability when overused. That is how it is with any EQ skill; it needs to be applied in balance and in sync with the use of our other skills.

Well used, flexibility can save you from road rage, unnecessary conflicts, and the wear and tear of resisting changes that you cannot control. Over done, flexibility might be the seed to grow conflict, adversity, and resentment. Being flexible doesn't mean allowing people to take advantage of you.

This chapter has addressed the complex and challenging implications change brings to our lives. We can be afraid of dragons breathing fire or any number of other challenges. Often flexibility is one of the best strengths to meet these difficulties. Notice how much flexibility helps your 2% Solution come about.

Here are some ways to grow your EQ skills in flexibility:

- Follow the well-known adage to "take one day at a time."

- Write a list of pros and cons when you are tempted to resist a change. Evaluate if your resistance will be valuable, and if so, how to exercise your resistance in a way that is respectful to you and others.

- Apply Stephen Covey's advice from *The 7 Habits of Highly Effective People* (1989) and expand your personal freedom by interrupting the automatic stimulus-response process and inserting a pause in the cycle (similar to counting to ten before responding in an argument). With the benefit of pausing, you determine the way you act, rather than have your past conditioning running the show.

2% in Motion

WELCOMING CHANGE

At age 45, Travis decided to change his over-stressed life. Motivated by this birthday, Travis decided he needed an effective and balanced life for his remaining years. He writes that, "Now at 60, I'm so glad I did!" Travis' 2% Project was to be trained by Stephen Covey in delivering the 7 Habits work. It has brought him peace of mind and satisfaction; it supports his mission of helping people and organizations achieve their best and perform at high standards. Travis enjoys the combined benefits of his professional work with his Al-Anon 12-Step men's group. He reports this lifelong project is teaching him humility and the importance of 12-Step slogans, such as "One day at a time" and "Progress, not perfection." Travis' engagement with his 2% Project led him to add focus by stating his lifelong 2% Solution, which is to give his gifts with energy while allowing time for peace and rest. His career evolution has taken him to the field of emotional intelligence, where he is excelling as a consultant who knows from personal experience that change is a part of the gift of the life process. ☯

....

PACE YOUR 2% PROCESS WITH EQ

Are you using your dexterity and flexibility as you are implementing your 2% Project? Look over your 2% implementation plan. Are any changes needed? Would your 2% Project be implemented better if you sharpened these skills? If so, write about your commitments to enhance your facility with these competencies in your 2% Journal.

Remember Travis' connection with the wisdom, "Progress, not perfection." When you pace yourself, you give the desired benefits natural time to unfold. This beautiful poem from the Bible, Ecclesiastes 3:1–8 is the best articulation I have heard of the importance of trusting that the natural unfolding of beauty will occur.

> *For everything there is a season,*
> *And a time for every matter under heaven:*
> *A time to be born, and a time to die;*
> *A time to plant, and a time to pluck up what is planted*

....

TUNE IN YOUR MIND

- Accept conflict and make it your ally, or as the Zen masters would say:

  EMBRACE TIGER; RETURN TO MOUNTAIN

- Grow your skills in flexibility. Allow yourself to be like a willow, able to bend in the wind but remain strong and sturdy.

- Face the dragons in your life with support from others and with a sense of humor.

- Resisting change and the accompanying pain can make the pain much worse. Let your heart break wide open and embrace the grieving and transition processes.

- Trust that you will find your answer along your well-lived journey.

. . . .

TUNE OUT THE NOISE

- Recognize the power perceptions play in your life. Be in charge; don't let them run your life.

- Avoid black-and-white thinking: that all change and conflict are either good or bad. It is a much more complex world. Use all the colors of the rainbow to understand your challenges.

- Don't let any animals hide in your closet or usurp your living room. Dragons don't belong in closets holding secrets, nor elephants in the living room trumpeting conflict. Tell the truth with compassion and by welcoming your support system.

. . . .

A SNEAK PREVIEW

Many factors influence the right choice for your 2% Project, including your age, life conditions, and generation. The next chapter will help you pinpoint the best project for you based on these dynamics in your life.

7 /

LEARNING FROM OTHERS
Pinpointing Your Personal 2% Solution

Seventeen-year-old Catherine made two mistakes, and according to the Catholic Church, they were two grave sins. She got pregnant as a single teen, and then she married outside the Catholic Church because it was the only way her new father-in-law would attend the wedding. When Catherine's daughter was born with one of her arms only partially developed and her parish priest refused to visit Catherine, she knew that God had abandoned her and that she was being punished through her innocent child. She made an immediate decision to be tough; not to ever let anyone hurt her daughter or her. Catherine closed herself off spiritually and emotionally and never talked about the pain for 32 long years. She also never forgot about it.

When she turned 50, Catherine finally decided it was time to heal. Her soul hungered for open spiritual engagement, and that hunger brought her secret out of the closet. She opened up and talked with her second husband, close friends in her church, and colleagues in her leadership group. Catherine developed a 2% Project based on reflection and action. She wrote in her journal, prayed, and walked. Movement was a vital part of her healing—moving by herself on a walk in the neighborhood or walking and talking with friends. Catherine's favorite form of reflection is in a group of trusted friends who take the time to listen with the ears of their hearts. The honest and caring feedback helps her tell the truth more fully and accept herself for whom she really is in response to the acceptance she experiences from others.

Catherine reflected as she told me her story, "Stifling emotions can be very destructive. I thought I was coping with everything very well, but the effects were evident in my demeanor, my unspoken sadness and seriousness. I was a good employee, but closed. I really missed the spiritual part of life. I definitely wanted to be in control, and I never believed that I really deserved anything better in life—I was my own worst enemy for 32 years. That's a lot of years to waste!"

Today Catherine is peacefully exuberant as she describes the joyous release and freedom that comes with feeling reborn. After 32 years of living under a dark, dry cloud, she initiated her liberating 2% Solution.

She's excited now when she talks about her recognition that she can change her brain and rebuild her thinking process. She's also committed to giving to her community. Catherine sees herself in the role of mentor, coach, and teacher for other women who may need similar encouragement and support. When we receive such gifts we often feel an imperative to share them, and Catherine still cannot stop herself from sharing her gifts freely with spontaneous heart-felt generosity...and she's tickled that she can't! (Because, of course, she doesn't want to.) She is becoming self-actualized through awareness, forgiving herself, and intentional action. %

Every stage of life brings new challenges. Catherine encountered a terrible challenge at 17, and in her 50s she used her life wisdom to transform her response to those events. Our challenges are colored by our beliefs, values, and life conditions. A GenXer just beginning a career has distinctly different interests and challenges than a Baby Boomer planning for retirement or getting ready to welcome a new grandchild. We are also influenced by our religious and spiritual preferences, our values, and our ethnicity. Many factors are always in play, interacting in fresh ways as the stages of your life change to guide and influence the evolution of your 2% Solution in a way that is completely unique to you. Those factors also exert tremendous influence over determining the perfect 2% Project for a particular time in your life. The 2% Project you construct at this moment will be distinct from ones that you'll create at later points in your life and is likely quite different from 2% Projects you may have done previously.

It's still true what Heraclitus said more than 2,500 years ago: "You could not step twice into the same river, for other waters are ever flowing on to you." Step into the river now. Let your 2% Solution and 2% Project reflect your life as it is right now. Let them guide you to fulfilling your core purpose.

In addition to your generation, many other factors influence your choice of a 2% Project. Women may have different personal goals from men. Your relationship to your career goals, your culture, your world views, and your values will appreciably influence the choice of the goals you pursue in your 2% Project. To help you determine the best mix of ingredients needed to achieve 100% of your 2% potential, this chapter outlines relevant research and illustrates differences with stories of a cross-section of women and men of various ages who have taken the 2% journey. Learn to:

- Factor into account your gender, generation, stage of life, and other prominent dynamics that influence the development of your 2% Solution and set the tone for your first 2% Project.

- Develop a better understanding of yourself and your co-workers by exploring how distinct constellations of values and self-identifying traits create apparently different segments of society.

- Find out about a whole new social group: the Cultural Creatives.

- Review and update your application of your 2% implementation plan.

- Build empathy to cross the apparent gaps that seem to separate us from one another.

....

TAKE YOUR 2% PULSE

When you are engaged with a process as valuable as designing your own 2% Solution, you need to consistently pay attention to the quality and truthfulness of your pursuit. This is not the place for little white lies, no matter how creative, and the 2% Solution is not for the feint of heart.

It is time to take the pulse of your 2% Process and gauge its strength. How well does your 2% Solution articulate your most important life intention? Is your 2% Process poised to supercharge the vision of your 2% Solution? Is any fine-tuning needed?

....

STAGES OF LIFE

In general, there are three dynamic stages of life that shape the 2% Project:

1. Young adult/Orienting your life

2. Mid-career/Mid-life

3. Advanced career/Embracing life

It is not surprising that there are specific types of projects that are most likely to come up in the three different phases of life. However, there are also some critical life conditions and events, such as depression, abuse, and addiction, that can demand attention at any time in your life.

We develop in fairly well-recognized broad stages of life, moving from infant to being a toddler, a child, an adolescent, and finally a young adult. Many wonderful sources explore the stages and transitions of the human lifecycles. Here, we will only focus on the internal and external pressures that may influence the selection of your 2% Projects. Because your big picture 2% Solution is designed to help you achieve a much larger and more general lifelong goal, it will incorporate and synthesize the more dramatic variations that will appear in your individual 2% Projects. Joan Borysenko asserts that life's cycles occur in seven-year periods. In *A Woman's Book of Life* (1996, 4), she writes:

> *I began to notice the theme of seven-year cycles in sources as varied as the work of C. G Jung, the Torah, the New Testament, the plays of Shakespeare, American folk wisdom, Native American tradition, Buddhist lore, the philosophy of the Greek mathematician Pythagoras, and naturally, in the phases of the moon that change every seventh day, and to which women's reproductive rhythms and hormonal pulses correspond.*

These seven-year cycles are likely to seem intuitively accurate to you. Think about your own life at various seven-year cycles, such as ages 21, 28, 35, and so on. Do a brief inventory of the seven-year cycles in your life by doing the following activity. Then review the information through reflecting as you answer the questions at the end of the exercise.

Activity: *The Jackpot: 7, 7, 7*

Contemplate your life according to key events; consider the things you learned and gained in each seven-year cycle of your life thus far. Some events and lessons will be really tough; some will be splendid. In the long run, they all join in the mix of creating the cake of your life.

For each seven-year block, list three major life events that occurred for you in this time frame, list three lessons you gained, and then list one other circumstance or event which feels important to you.

Here is the strategy to sketch out in your 2% Journal.

Your Age	0–7	8–14	15–21	22–28	29–35	36–42	43–49	50–56	57–63	63–70+

1. Circumstance

2. Circumstance

3. Circumstance

4. Lesson

5 Lesson

6 Lesson

7 Other

Now, put this in perspective by answering the following questions:

Are there patterns? Did you have any key "ah-ha" insights? What does this tell you about your strengths that you can draw on to realize your 2% Solution? What weaknesses, challenges, or flash points should you be aware of and avoid?

Of course, your personal circumstances, in addition to your age, will influence what constitutes the best 2% Projects to support your growth. The following three clusters of stories illustrate typical issues, demands, and expectations that arise in the different stages of life and some 2% Projects that address those challenges.

Young Adult/Orienting Your Life: 21 to 35

Young adults are typically focused on wrapping up their formal education, bursting onto the career scene, and living free and easy while also considering relationships and defining where home is going to be. The world is often their playground. They have high energy, enjoy a good time, and are sketching out other plans. They may be skiing, hiking, traveling, and participating in sports, all while they are beginning to commit to long-term responsibilities in relationships at home, at work, and in the community. By the time they reach the end of this age cluster, they have enjoyed a certain amount of success and struggled with their share of challenges, and most have begun to seek the deeper meaning that lies beyond the routine sorrows and satisfactions of life. They find themselves asking the classic question posed in the popular movie, "What's it all about, Alfie?"

2% in Motion

RUNNING FOR HER LIFE

In her 20s and just out of an undergraduate program in London, Rhonda decided to spend a few years working before beginning work on her Ph.D. Though she was already living a fast-paced life with her new career, she decided to kick things into high gear by training for a marathon. She was not an experienced runner, but the challenge tantalized her and she turned it into a 2% Project. Rhonda had always been rewarded for her thinking; she had been so busy using her head that she seldom had time to develop the rest of herself. It was a courageous step for her to move out of her comfort zone and focus on a big physical challenge, but she was ready for something very different.

Besides attaining a high level of fitness, she received a couple of unexpected perks from training. She discovered that her improved cardiovascular strength boosted her overall efficiency and significantly increased her happiness. Today this wisdom is still serving her while she is completing her Ph.D. and working at the United Nations. Rhonda wants to help bring economic stabilization to the world's pocr—a big goal. She learned how to engage her whole self when she trained for and ran a marathon; now she's going to engage her whole self in her continuing quest for justice. %

2% in Motion

ONE STEP AT A TIME

Tanya spent months working to identify her 2% Solution. Her first efforts produced a few ideas of what she needed to work on, but her inner goal didn't crystallize until she recognized that her overall solution was "To accept and love myself." In emotional intelligence terms, Tanya had realized the value of fully developing a healthy self-regard by learning to accept herself, warts and all.

Her first 2% Project was to forgive, accept, and love her father. She had felt alienated from him since her parents' divorce and she was sure he didn't love her.

Tanya started working with a therapist, wrote extensively in her journal, doing her best to piece together all the memories she was able to recall about her father. Gradually she began to reach out to him, first in writing and then by talking on the phone, until they finally met in person. They took a long walk, and standing by a beautiful lake, they were finally able to bridge the gap of all those years; he was able to reassure her that he had always loved her.

Tanya knew her 2% Solution would be a lifelong process, and she patiently moved ahead one step at a time. Her next step was to end an unhealthy relationship that she had allowed to drag on for four years. After completing that step, another man at work began to harass her sexually, but the self-confidence she had acquired gave her the strength to confront this challenge directly and effectively. Tanya moved through challenge after challenge with strength and consistency, and will continue to do so, because she sees everything that comes up as a part of her life goal to love and accept herself.

She portrays her 2% Process as a rosebud starting to open up, and as it continues to open, it reveals a spiral reaching to her inner core. %

If you are in the 21–35 stage of orienting your life, be sure to consider how the effects of your 2% Solution might extend far into the future. Let it become the beacon for your life's work. Choose this 2% Project, and each subsequent one, in a way that will complement your current stage of life and build to the next. You will often need to remind yourself to be patient. At every stage of life most of us want to get things done *now*, but the more mature we become, the more we understand why that simply isn't possible. Life is a transition—a process—and it requires great patience as it unfolds.

Another tip is to make your 2% Project fun; this will make it easier to honor your commitment to keep at it. It's the idea found in step 9 of the Action Plan (see Chapters 2 and 4). Of course, things won't always go perfectly. You'll get sidetracked once in awhile, but if you miss a time you have scheduled to work on your project, forgive yourself, renew your commitment, and move forward. Feeling guilty is an unproductive state to remain in—and a seductive one at that. The poem "Desiderata" counsels us, "...beyond a wholesome discipline, be gentle with yourself," and Rainer Maria Rilke advises patience in *Letters to a Young Poet* (1984, 34):

> *Have patience with everything unresolved in your heart and try to love the questions themselves as if they were locked rooms or books written in a very foreign language. Don't search for the answers, which could not be given to you now, because you would not be able to live them. And the point is, to live everything. Live the questions now. Perhaps then, someday far in the future, you will gradually, without even noticing it, live your way into the answer.*

Mid-Career/Mid-Life: 36 to 49

Riches and challenges are typical of the mid-career/mid-life stage. Jung believed that every midlife crisis is a spiritual crisis. Whether or not you would characterize your challenges during this part of your life as spiritual, they probably carry some deeper meaning. In some ways you are an archeologist on an expedition to uncover the true meaning in your life. The 2% Solution helps you find the place to dig; your 2% Projects are your tools.

For many, the focus on children is a central theme during this stage. For some it means bringing their first child into the world; for others it is coping with learning that they cannot have children. Still others are older birds facing an empty nest. Aside from children, many are taking their careers to the pinnacle during this time. Other typical events include increasing volunteer or community responsibilities, purchasing a home or moving to a larger one, and possibly becoming part of the sandwich generation—taking care of children and aging parents. Whew! It's a big, big time. That is why so many women and men in this cluster are doing deep soul-searching.

The depth of the questions and searching deepens for most from "What's it all about, Alfie?" to "How do I lead a simplified, meaningful, and fully *authentic* life?" How, indeed? Let's look at a few 2% Projects that some deeply inquiring people have used to explore this question. In their own ways, each of the people I have talked with who are experiencing the mid-career/mid-life stage took on the struggle to accept themselves as good enough, and then they had to learn how to assert their skills with appropriate authority. This is all a part of the unfolding to become your authentic self.

2% in Motion

FIRST-AID FOR THE SOUL

Benjamin has struggled all his life with the problem of negative self-talk. Finally, at age 40, he became so tired of the little voices in his head constantly questioning his worth and his actions that he decided to initiate a 2% Solution to "improve my self-confidence." It always helps to name a dragon, and Benjamin breathed a sigh of relief when he told me how much just naming this issue had helped him.

Next he started to work on his goal of being willing to take more risks and stop criticizing himself so much. He used Albert Ellis' Rational Emotive Training process to create cognitive counters to the negative messages he was giving himself. For example, if an internal critic asked, "Dummy, why did you say that to the boss?"

he'd counter with "The boss knows I am seeking to take more initiative and propose new ideas. She is supportive." Benjamin accepts that this is going to take continual effort, but that was almost a deal-breaker for him at the start. It was a daunting challenge to think he would have to be vigilant for the rest of his life. He had thought he could recognize his issue, erase it, and go merrily along with his life. Unfortunately, life is rarely that simple. Yet as a result of his persistence the scope of his courage keeps expanding. Benjamin decided to take a risk and created a new business in marketing, which is now sailing forth successfully. %

> Nobody can make you feel inferior without your consent.
>
> —Eleanor Roosevelt

2% in Motion

A COMMITMENT TO SELF

In her mid-forties, depression brought Candace to her knees. Until then it hadn't been so bad; it just reared its ugly head in small containable circumstances. Then, when her business partners didn't want to include her in their new business and her mother died, she crawled into bed. She almost withered away there.

Fortunately, Candace has the gift of developing deep friendships. Those friends showed up and insisted that Candace get up and go to work. She cut and styled hair, gave perms, and shared wisdom. Seldom did she talk about how difficult her struggle was, but the minute she got out of the salon and on all the other days, Candace went to bed.

It turned out Candace had an ace up her sleeve—commitment. She had made a commitment to be a part of a golf foursome on Tuesday mornings, and she kept that commitment. Candace reflected, "No one judges you on the golf course. No one cares how you play as long as you keep up. During the depression I made myself go every Tuesday to my foursome because they were 'my girls' and I couldn't let them down. They depended on me. Commitment is essential to

*me; it's a personal connection which is huge for me. What's impor-
tant is you don't have to make anyone else happy with golf. And it's
very humbling; I knew I couldn't be perfect."*

*Her 2% Project, golf on Tuesday, took 3½ hours a week, 2% of
her time. That was both a big and life-saving commitment for Candace. Ultimately, she came to recognize that accepting herself and
living up to core commitments is her life's 2% Solution. With the help
of therapy, medication for a while, great friends, and staying active
through her commitments, Candace pulled out of her depression.
Now she knows how to keep her spirits up, and through her ongoing
2% Solution Candace continues to play golf and keep her personal
friendships vibrant.* %

A DEFINING MOMENT

Your "simple" challenge, the one that doesn't seem nearly profound
enough, may be exactly the ticket to your personal home run.

Each of these stories has illustrated the challenging and inspiring
trek toward becoming genuinely alive. You can get there, too. All it takes
is 2% of your time and 100% of your personal honesty and willingness.
These stories demonstrate the tremendous challenge and opportunity
we experience from 36 to 49.

Advanced Career/Embracing Life: 50 to 63+

From 50 through the rest of your life is admittedly (and hopefully) a *big*
time span. The roles we fill in this stage will be numerous and diversi-
fied. Some are still parenting at the beginning of this life stage; others are
grandparents. Some are excelling in their careers and just about to step
up to a senior executive position; others are starting their own business,
which they will operate at a slower pace; others are retiring. Diversity
reigns, yet there are common threads. The importance of connecting
meaning and action in their lives is unequivocal. The commitment to
simplicity and the value of deep and caring relationships grows.

For many, the most important focus is their increasing spiritual or
religious development. Rabbi Zalman Schachter-Shalomi's book *From*

Age-ing to Sage-ing (1997) is a good resource for learning more about how to make this the best time of your life. You may want to develop your 2% Solution around one of his suggestions. Here are a few stories to demonstrate the use of the 2% Process to gain more from these years of harvest and new beginnings.

2% in Motion

EXPANDING CREATIVITY

Fifty-something-year-old Carmen created a 2% Solution to nurture her creativity in preparation for the transitions in her life. It evolved over time to combine with her focus on spirituality; she would go inside herself, let go, and empty, "so the Great Spirit could flow in." Carmen bought a set of cassettes of her favorite poetry and listened to them as she drove. She deepened her meditative prayer practice and wrote in her journal. She sought to open to her creativity through her writing.

Carmen reports that her project increased her strong desire for balance and giving less to work and more to her personal life, though she still occasionally struggles to implement the balance. Her 2% Solution has given more value to her life. She says, "My aspirations are different; I seek more depth, peace, simplicity." Typical of others in this stage of life, integrating purpose and value has freed Carmen to act in greater accordance with what is important to her and to worry less about approval from others. Carmen explained that what started out as a 2% Project has become her strategy for her Life's 2% Solution. %

2% in Motion

ACT WITH INTENTION

David was 50, retired from the military, and an IT director for a large transportation company when he started his 2% Solution to act more in accord with his whole self, instead of letting habit dictate action. His first 2% Project was to redirect his priorities to his family. He knew it was time to give up the typical male way of life where his wife and children took a backseat to his needs. He gained a great

deal of joy and support as he shared his life and the family responsibilities in new ways.

Then David was ready to take on his second 2% Project, which
was harder for him. He intended to get and stay in better physical
health. David was considerably overweight and couldn't see how
spending 2% of his time on this worry would cut his waistline. Turns
out his Project was actually a lifeline. He discovered the South Beach
Diet and lost 60 pounds between his birthday in August and Christ-
mas. Now he exercises regularly and stays committed to maintaining
his awareness on all fronts—from what he eats to how he interacts
with his family. David advises that "if the desire is there, you can accomplish hard things." %

Each of these people have cried and laughed their way through the
2% Project that brought more value and meaning to their lives. They
wouldn't give up their growth for anything.

TALKIN' 'BOUT MY GENERATION

I can hear the late '60s Guess Who tune by this title in my head as I
write. That gives me away as a Boomer (but you likely figured that out
long ago). In addition to your age and your stage in life, there is another
aspect of timing that will influence your selection of your 2% Solution. The historical generation in which we were born also significantly
influences our preferences. Strengthening the EQ skill of empathy can
help you work and play better with others of any generation.

The bottom line for the many generational differences is that it represents one aspect of yourself to consider as you fully engage in your
life. If any of these areas of classic differences, such as work ethic, are a
sore point for you, consider how your 2% Solution relates to that rub.
If you are a GenXer and you want to work—but not too much—your
2% Solution might relate to accomplishing that balance. As a part of
the implementation of your project, you might include expressing empathy toward those of other generations who don't understand your

boundaries, or you might challenge yourself to develop a friendship with someone from every different generation to increase your empathy and understanding. *Vive la différence!*

If you're a Boomer, think back to how your parents seemed when you were young and how you swore you'd never become an old fogey like them. The people from Generations X and Y grew up on the same planet as you, but they grew up in different worlds. They are somewhat hip to yours, but you may be almost oblivious to theirs. See if you can be cool enough for them to give you a tour.

OTHER INFLUENCES ON YOUR 2% SELECTION

Other factors in your life influence how resiliently you cope with the day-to-day wins and losses of your life. While they could ultimately influence the creation of your 2% Solution, they are even more likely to influence the right 2% Project for you at this time in your life. Reviewing these factors also can help you recognize when it is time to start a new 2% Project because some critical elements in your life have shifted or simply because you have grown. Areas to consider include:

- *Gender*—What aspects of being a man or woman affect your sense of purpose and your relationship with others?

- *Personality factors*—If you know your Myers-Briggs or your Emergenetics profile, or have other measurements of how to understand yourself, use that information for all its worth. You can use this "data" to influence the way you design and implement your 2% Projects and your life long 2% Solution.

- *Values*—Your most important values will greatly influence your global 2% Solution. They will guide you to center your attention on what is truly most important to your heart and help you balance your time between inner and outer demands. Combine the information you gained about values with your generational and stage-of-life concerns to help you design a project that resonates with your worldview. Additionally, consider the Cultural Creatives approach (discussed later in this chapter).

- *Family needs and obligations, addiction, mental health challenges*—Each of these areas can seriously impact your life, requiring that they be dealt with first.

- *Spiritual/religious*—The importance of your spiritual practice or your religious beliefs is likely to affect everything you do, including your 2% Process.

A DEFINING MOMENT

A quarter of the population of the United States and Europe are "Cultural Creatives."

Cultural Creatives

What we value manifests as our identity. In addition to the integrated-values thinking from Spiral Dynamics, there is another way to approach this same idea, which Paul Ray distilled from market surveys he conducted. Thirteen-plus years of gathering data led him to recognize the emergence of a new subculture in the United States. By the 1990s, he and co-author Sherry Ruth Anderson named the group the Cultural Creatives (CCs), because they saw the new cluster was "literally creating a new culture in America" (*The Cultural Creatives*, (2000, *xi*). Ray received grants from several organizations to conduct large surveys. These, and the subsequent 60 interviews he and co-author Anderson conducted, created a substantial database demonstrating the development of an entire new subculture in the United States.

The authors site research in other parts of the world that corroborate the same development. For example, they report that "Officials of the European Union, hearing of the numbers of Cultural Creatives in the United States, launched a related survey in each of the fifteen countries in September 1997," finding at least as many CCs across Europe as in the U.S. (5).

Just as with Spiral Dynamics integral (SDi), the research identifying this cultural change focused on understanding the "values and worldviews that shape people's lives—the deep structure that shifts gradually. . .[because] values are the best single predictor of real behavior" (7). It is true that values change slowly, but they do shift. That is how societal evolution happens. Staying in tune with yourself through reality testing, meditation, journaling, and reflective contemplation will help you sense if your values are beginning to shift. . . and such a shift calls for re-evaluating your 2% Solution. Ask yourself if it needs to tweaked or totally revised. Ray and Anderson found that the people they labeled as Cultural Creatives actually "changed their substrate of values, and they may be reshaping it in our larger culture as well."

The authors identify three cultures in the U.S.: the Traditionals, the Moderns, and the Cultural Creatives. As of 1999, Traditionals were 24.5 percent of the United Sates population—48 million adults. Most have low incomes and a high school education or less and seldom vote. Some of the values and beliefs this group espouses include that men and women should keep their traditional roles, patriarchs should dominate the family, the conservative version of their own religious traditions should be upheld, sexuality should not be discussed openly, women are generally expected to follow the leadership of men, and sexual behavior should be strictly regulated by religious doctrine, laws, and moral codes They prefer to see the world in black-and-white categories to ensure more certainty (30–32).

The Moderns constitute almost half of the U.S. population and are quite diverse, including large numbers of liberals and conservatives and nearly all income levels. The authors note, "Read *Time, The New York Times, The Wall Street Journal, Business Week, Forbes*, or *USA Today*, and you will get the official ideology laid out in detail" (25). As of 1999, Moderns were about 93 million of the 193 million adults in the U.S., and they represented the same diversity as general demographics showed throughout the United States. They believe hook, line, and sinker in the technological economy. This belief system is over 500 years old, beginning around the time of the Renaissance. These are the people who gained power for the first time by fighting off the traditional church, clan, and economic structures.

Some of the values they hold dear (27) include making or having a lot of money, being successful, looking good, having lots of choices, supporting technological development, and acting as if time is money.

This may remind you of the point made with Spiral Dynamics in Chapter 2: you cannot identify someone's preferred value cluster by their age or generation. While this may seem surprising, note that we are looking at the deeper inner structures of how we decide what is important. Hopefully, you have been working throughout this book to clarify your values. Now think of others who share those values; within that group you can probably identify people who are of different ages, genders, generations, and have socioeconomic differences.

The values of the CCs include perseverance, the capability to reflect deeply, and open-mindedness. Authenticity is increasingly being waved around as the flag to rally Cultural Creatives. Ray and Anderson report that CCs have two ways of learning: (1) personal experience

> You can't shake hands with a clenched fist.
>
> —Indira Gandhi

and (2) a wide view of the big picture of all the relevant factors affecting the world. Being aware of the vast spectrum of interrelationships is of great importance.

Concerns generally labeled as women's issues are important to all CCs—men and women alike. Those issues include feeling empathy for others, being against violence toward women and children, and making environmentally sustainable decisions. The authors identify two components of the Cultural Creatives. The Core CCs were about 24 million people in 1999 in the U.S., and there were twice as many women than men. In addition to the values just described, Core CCs place great importance on personal growth and spirituality. The other part of the CC group is labeled the Green CCs, and their values are more externally focused on the environment, relationships, and social matters. This group was about 26 million strong and had equal numbers of men and women in 1999.

Self-actualization, the emotional intelligence skill we have been exploring throughout our 2% work, is a much higher value to the CCs than the population at large. For example, the authors found that 60 percent of the U.S. population at large agrees with "the belief that every person has a unique gift to offer while 90% of CCs hold this belief. They also highly value the importance of discovering new things about themselves, expanding their creativity, and "developing more self awareness—that is, not sleepwalking through life" (191).

Form a sense of the group with which you most closely associate. You can do that by rereading these brief summaries, reading the book *Cultural Creatives*, or looking at the website at *www.culturalcreatives. com*. If you haven't already formed a sense of where your center of gravity resides from the Spiral Dynamics discussion in Chapter 2, the following cross-reference might help. The breakdown articulated by Ray and Anderson bears a substantial relationship to SDi; they use three instead of eight categories because they aren't seeking to categorize all the stages of human values development that have occurred throughout history. Notice that some areas will overlap because of the differences in the way the two systems view the developmental process.

Ray and Anderson	Spiral Dynamics integral
Traditional	Blue
Modern	Orange, Green
Green Cultural Creative	Green
Core Cultural Creative	Yellow, Turquoise

When you understand how these value patterns emerge and influence human behavior, and with which clusters you resonate most deeply, your personal clarity makes it much easier for you to act authentically. This facilitates feeling that you are truly walking your

Movements begin when people refuse to live divided lives.

—Ray and Anderson (20) (attributing the statement to educator Parker Palmer)

talk. Fortunately, grasping these types of values will also help you understand what motivates others and will help improve your relationships with people who seem different.

Engage Your EQ: *Empathy*

Whatever systems guide us individually, we are on this planet together and we implement our 2% Solutions in a community. Consequently, the emotional intelligence skill highlighted in this chapter is empathy, which is a critical component of your social intelligence, your persuasive capabilities, and your personal effectiveness. Perfect this skill and your life will be better at home and at work—guaranteed!

What's in it for you to express empathy and thus develop good relationships? Why care? Aren't you too busy, anyway? Write out your thoughts in your 2% Journal.

Empathy is based on caring about and understanding the feelings of others. You reflect your ability to exercise empathy when you are able to accurately read other people's emotions and use that information to help them feel understood and appreciated. If you strongly disagree with a coworker's assessment of a situation, you draw on your skills in empathy to first acknowledge his or her feelings and how important those feelings are. Only after that do you express your differing perspective. You will be much more persuasive and develop much better relationships using this skill.

Seven percent of communication comes from the spoken word (including e-mail), an additional 38 percent is gained when we hear the tonality of the communication (including voice-mail), and a whopping 55 percent of the information we receive comes from nonverbal cues, which can only be conveyed when we are in each others' physical presence. We exercise increasingly effective empathy when we learn to read people's nonverbal cues. Those messages will come in a zillion ways—or almost. It will be in skin tone, posture, tension, facial expressions, hand movements, and more. Your ticket to gaining a great deal of ground in your communications is to pause and notice. Ask your intuition, or your heart brain and your gut wisdom, for guidance. To be consciously aware of what they notice, you'll have to stop and ask.

Some useful empathy skills:

- Stand and deliver. Be accountable to yourself. Decide how important relationships with others are to you. Also decide how empathetic you want to be. Then take time to walk your talk.

- Refresh your etiquette. Create a working and community environment that encourages respect, understanding, and consideration.

- Freeze. Pause, notice, and learn from all the nonverbal cues you receive.

- Walk a mile or two in someone else's footwear. Listen with the ears of your heart—and with your whole mind.

- Use a wide-angle lens. Be open-minded in your discussions. Trust yourself enough to have the flexibility to listen well to others.

TARGET PRACTICE

You were first invited to fill out the Action Plan for your 2% Project in Chapter 2, and then asked to add your reflective processes in Chapter 4. We are well down the road now, and throughout this chapter we focused on elements of identity that will help you choose the 2% Solution with the most impact. Certainly, it is time to see whether you are on target. Turn to your Action Plan, your 2% Journal, or whatever will help you evaluate your progress. Ask yourself these questions as you check out your ten steps:

- Steps 1 and 2: Have you found the right 2% Solution and the appropriate 2% Project to implement at this point in your life? Having just further considered the impacts of your stage of life, generation, values, and other factors, are there any changes or fine-tuning that will bring you to greater clarity?

- Step 3: How are you exercising your reflecting muscles? Are you becoming increasingly aware of how you are living your life?

- Step 4: Do you have a functional routine so that you are effectively spending 2% of your time every week on your project?

- Step 5: What is happening as you are implementing your 2% Project? Is there anything new? Stay alert.

- Steps 6 and 7: Have you recently imagined the results from carrying out your 2% Project for six months? Make a list of the situations and ways in which you will be seen differently. Write down the new things that you will hear people say that reflect on how differently you will be feeling and record your reflections.

- Step 8: Who are your mentors and others giving you meaningful feedback as you are growing?

- Steps 9 and 10: By all means, be certain that you are loving the rewards from your project along the way. Are you having fun? Can you tell you are increasingly singing your song—or at least getting closer to your song?

TUNE IN YOUR MIND

- Identify your generation and other critical factors in your life to be certain you are getting focused on your own unique 2% Project.

- Decide which cultural group fits you—Traditionals, Moderns, or Cultural Creatives. Clarifying the answer to this question can help you know yourself more fully, understand others you associate with, and most importantly, walk your talk.

- Regularly check in with your 2% implementation plan. Keep yourself on target.

- Expand your emotional and social intelligence through spending time with your friends and strengthening your relationships. Take time to read and respond to people's nonverbal cues.

....
TUNE OUT THE NOISE

- Avoid valuing paper and tasks over significant others in your life.

- Do not think that your life is on one continuous role with no breaks. Pay attention to the stage of life you are in right now. What do you need to do—*now*?

- Miss nonverbal cues at your own peril. When possible, talk with someone instead of sending an e-mail. Pay attention to the other person instead of yourself during a conversation.

....
A SNEAK PREVIEW

Chapter 8 explores employing your whole brain—head, heart, and belly—to think, decide, and act. Left and right brain differences are explored. Link whole-mind thinking and action with the full four dimensions of yourself and expand your emotional intelligence skills of problem-solving.

8/

ZAP THE MAP
Integrate Your Mind, Body, and Soul

Sharon was a high-level manager, and she loved blending her engineering and people skills on the job daily. She was outgoing and upbeat, and her genuine caring for her staff and colleagues was one of her signature attributes. Connecting with friends at work was integral to her job satisfaction.

She left work early for a checkup with her obstetrician; she was expecting her first child and couldn't be happier. Her world spun out of control that afternoon when the amniocentesis showed her first child had a genetic predisposition for Turner Syndrome, a rare chromosomal disorder in females with a broad range of symptoms, from heart defects to loss of ovarian function to shortness of stature.

Sharon and her husband were advised by the doctor not to tell anyone so the baby wouldn't be labeled. Her anguish bottled up, Sharon turned her fury on God—how could he let this happen? To make matters worse, she felt increasingly ambivalent about their decision not to tell anyone. Sharon was an external processor and she felt alienated keeping her distress inside.

Fortunately, she joined a leadership group where she worked on her 2% Project "to recapture and enhance her spirituality," and things have become brighter and brighter. Her project led her to participate more actively in her church and talk with trusted friends to come out of her isolation. She reversed her previous decision and told her church group and close friends about her daughter, and they have been a great source of support. They were invaluable in help-ing her reflect and work through her concerns and anxiety. Sharon did more than ponder, pray, and talk about it. She engaged with all domains of her being—body, mind, heart, and soul. Physically, she exercised regularly and ate a nutritious, well-balanced diet. Men-tally she sought facts and information, which gave her a deeper un-derstanding of the condition and allowed her to gain some perspec-tive, which she hadn't been able to do when the concern was being shoved underground. Emotionally, she sought comfort and support from friends and colleagues. And spiritually she turned to her church and to her God. %

Think back to the classic film *The Wizard of Oz*. The Scarecrow wanted the Wizard to give him a fistful of gray matter so he could be smart. Lit-tle did he know he had other brains, and so do you. While what goes on between the ears is important, there is much more to using your whole mind than engaging the gray matter. Sharon engaged her whole mind to find what was troubling her and explore the right answers. She drew on the skills valued by the whole cast of characters—the Scarecrow, the Lion, and the Tin Man. Like Dorothy, she was seeking her true home, which meant she needed to forgive herself and come fully alive.

It's time to stop confusing the brain with the mind. Scientists have proven what intuitive individuals have always sensed: The mind incor-porates all your awareness, not just what happens in the skull. While the brain resides in the head, other parts of the body influence awareness, decision-making, and more—a network of neurotransmitters connect-ing the brain to the heart and the gut produce emotional and physical responses.

Developing a truly effective 2% Solution requires using the mind, heart, and gut—the analytical and intuitive selves. Research by the In-stitute of HeartMath reveals that there is dynamic, two-way commu-nication between the brain and the heart, with each influencing the other's function. Avoid brain drain and embrace this chapter to learn how to:

- Employ your whole brain to think, decide, and act.

- Understand your right-brain/left-brain preferences and how that colors your world.

- Consider taking a profile to understand which thinking and behaving preferences you will build on as you work with your whole mind.

- Work with ways of perceiving how you construct your maps of reality.

- Link whole-mind thinking and action with emotional intelligence, particularly the skill of problem solving.

······································

INTEGRAL THINKING

A core requirement for authentic living is *integral thinking*, which means bringing together the different parts of your thinking into a composite whole. The term *integral* is commonly defined as "having nothing omitted or taken away: lacking nothing that belongs to it" and refers to words such as *complete*, *entire*, and *perfect*. We will focus on the concepts of complete and entire, because perfectionism is only good for crazy-making. But it is just as crazy to think, act, and decide with only part of our database.

Learning to use your whole brain often requires discovering aspects of internal wisdom that you didn't even know existed. Because it's impossible to honor a part of yourself you don't know, integral thinking begins with a discovery process. Discerning the whispering voices within yourself that have been unnoticed or unheeded for years requires discipline and patience... but maybe even more importantly, it requires curiosity and courage, as the Lion in *The Wizard of Oz* knew so well.

The brain encompasses much more than what is inside the head. We have neurotransmitters all over our body. Candace Pert, in her groundbreaking book *Molecules of Emotion* (1997), states that we have memory in every cell of our body—yes, every cell! Others tell us there is a second brain around our hearts and that there are more than 100 million neurons in a person's gut.

So think about it—at every moment you are being flooded with information from multiple sources. It is a lot to pull together, and to gain all this wisdom, you will need to give yourself the chance to wonder, "What else might I know below the surface that I haven't let my conscious mind in on yet?"

The brain is wider than the sky
For, put them side by side
The one the other will include
With ease, and you beside.

—Emily Dickenson, Collected Poems

A DEFINING MOMENT

What do butterflies in your stomach and common sense have in common? They are both your silent teachers—listen.

THE BELLY BRAIN

Dean Radin, author of *The Conscious Universe* (1997), is quoted in the May–July 2004 issue of *What Is Enlightenment* as finding that "research results support growing evidence that humans do have more than one brain... And the belly brain...seems to have responses and 'feelings' that are all its own. In fact, it might sometimes have a different take on things than big brother upstairs."

But you already know this. Think about those times when all the facts suggest you would be a fool to do anything but "choice A," although your gut is screaming not to do it. That, my friend, is your belly brain in action.

As an example, a colleague and her partner were interviewing to hire a new office manager. The partner eagerly identified one of the candidates as the hands-down favorite. She had the best resumé, the most experience, and good references. Although all the facts pointed to a slam-dunk decision, my colleague felt alarm bells going off inside her gut. Yet, she acquiesced to her partner because she didn't have "one good reason" to oppose the choice except this bad-belly feeling. She called the candidate to offer her the job, which was readily accepted. A month later the newly employed manager was asked to leave. It was a terrible fit.

If those two co-workers had been able to incorporate that bad-belly feeling into the mix when they were making their decision, they would have spared themselves and the person they mistakenly hired some serious heartburn and sleepless nights. Belly, or gut, knowledge is a part of our wisdom, and we need to be aware of it, value it, and use it.

Often this gut wisdom is called *intuition*. Belly brain, intuition, gut feeling—call it what you will; they all point to the same thing. Current research, such as that being conducted by Gary Klein, author of *The Power of Intuition* (2004), is demonstrating that there is a rational process supporting this gut wisdom. We just haven't known how to interpret it. Klein's research, reviewed in an article by Breen in the September 2000 issue of *Fast Company*, found that people like firefighters and nurses, who make split-second life-or-death decisions, use a different decision-making process than most people. Typically, people are advised to approach decision-making by first evaluating, then developing criteria and considering multiple options before making a rational choice.

Klein also found that such a process wasn't ideal for all decisions. The problem is that it's often too slow and it leaves out other key sources of information. Emergency decision-makers make an initial decision and then, Klein says, run it "through a mental simulation. They imagine how a course of action may unfold and how it may ultimately play out. The process is akin to building a sequence of snapshots, and then observing what occurs."

Step 6 of the 2% Project Action Plan includes this strategy (see Chapters 2 and 4 for more on the 10-Step Action Plan). It calls for you to imagine your anticipated results. Another way to refer to this process is with a term from neurolinguistic programming terminology: *future pacing*. With this technique you use all your senses—visual, auditory, and kinesthetic—to build that sequence of snapshots.

With future pacing, you use your wisdom, reason, and intuition to check out the viability of your project. It lets you fine-tune your direction early instead of wasting time and energy going down the wrong path. It's a way of putting your crystal ball to good use! For example, if your 2% Solution is to reintroduce creativity into your life, and you decide to begin with a 2% Project of playing the piano for 30 minutes a day, you can envision the effectiveness of this project. You would imagine that it is six months down the road and you have been faithfully playing the piano. You may even have an image of your level of competence. How do you feel? Are you satisfied, nourished, replenished, or is this just another task you're supposed to do?

In your imagination, listen to yourself play. Pretend you are describing your progress to a close friend and pay attention to your tonality. How does your voice sound? Are you happy or just dragging along? Finally, check out how you feel, perhaps in your belly or by your breathing. What tactical senses do you have about playing the piano? Do you feel excited and creative or just ho-hum? This is valuable data. Remember to use it!

> Whether or not you acknowledge your gut reactions, they are shaping everything you do, just as they shape everything that everyone around you does. . . all the time.
>
> —Robert Cooper, *The Other 90%* (2001, 16)

LEADING FROM THE HEART

Daniel Goleman, probably the most recognized name in the world of emotional intelligence, describes the four key structures of emotional intelligence as: (1) being able to understand our emotions, (2) being able to manage our emotions, (3) being able to understand the emotions of others, and (4) being able to manage the emotions of others. As you learn to listen more deeply to your heart through your 2% Solution, you will more effectively manage your emotions and balance your life.

While this may initially seem like a big assertion, just think about this from your own experience. The fact that you are striving for a 2%

Solution demonstrates that you already have a sense that working with your heart is the power point for your emotional engagement.

As Doc Childre and Howard Martin, authors of *The HeartMath Solution* (1999), write, "Institute scientists have found that when subjects focus in the heart area and activate a core heart feeling such as love, appreciation, or care, this focus immediately shifts their heart rhythms. When the rhythms become more coherent, a cascade of neural and biochemical events begins that affects virtually every organ in the body" (15).

Your 2% Project, especially as supported by your reflective process, should lead you to experience this coherence between your heart and your mind. Integrating the wisdom from your whole being means you will draw on your heart, mind, body, and soul. No matter how the neuroscientists might specifically define it, this is an integration of your sensory, cognitive, and emotional information processing capabilities. When acting in accordance with your heart's deepest desire, this integration will naturally be happening for you. Additionally, following the 10-Step Action Plan for your 2% Project as described in Chapter 2 will facilitate that integration; in particular, by working with Step 5 to implement your project; Steps 6 and 7 to imagine your results and make changes if necessary; and Step 8 in receiving reflection from others influential to you.

2% in Motion

100% SUCCESS WITH 2%
Karen was a successful financial and technical writer for a well-known media company. Throughout her life she had struggled with the fear of not fitting in—fears that were reinforced by her own childhood experience. A raucous choir of self-doubts plagued her. One of her leadership group friends referred to those self-imposed critics as her "internal committee." Wherever they came from, they kept Karen thinking in her head and steering clear of her heart.

She frequently found that she had a different point of view, but she muffled it, along with her internal critics, and fit in just fine. Over time Karen recognized that those critical voices would always be a part of her, so she decided to implement a 2% Project that would put their criticism in perspective.

Karen began to voice her different opinions, she slowly recognized her value and became an active contributor to company strategy. She took her project further and blossomed with it—she has been writing a business humor column for several years now in a nationally recognized newspaper. Her next goal is to become nationally syndicated.

It is the deep longing that Karen felt that helped her find the momentum to challenge her old way of life. It wasn't easy, and she had to craw on her whole brain—head, heart, and belly. She didn't want to rock the boat, make waves, or appear too crazy, but she was going to give her whole self a voice. Because of her courage, she brought a new voice to public dialog, and. Karen is now a rising star in her field. Her sphere of influence increased enormously because of a 2% Project with a simple goal of speaking out that she initiated seven years ago. Karen has reaped great rewards by incorporating her 2% Project as a permanent part of her life, recognizing that it will change over time. %

POLITICS ASIDE

Regardless of one's political leanings, when it comes to brain activity we all must value both the right and the left. Roger Sperry won a Nobel Prize in 1981 for his research on the brain. He was a lead researcher in identifying the key functions associated with the left and right hemispheres of the brain. The left side of the brain brings the skills of analytical thinking and provides the basis for oral and written language. These are the skills most tested by the Wechsler IQ test, and because for so many decades we treated these as the only or the best ways to be smart, the left side of the brain has often been treated as the dominant side. Yet, the right brain is every bit as valuable. The right brain works in a more abstract and holistic fashion. As Andrew Newberg, Eugene

D'Aquili, and Vince Rause describe in *Why God Won't Go Away* (2001), right-brain thinking also includes visual-spatial perceptions and expression of our emotions.

Understanding how we use both sides of our brain is fundamental to making good choices in our life. When your life feels fragmented or robotic, consider whether you are drawing on both sides of your brain. The bottom line is you must use all your skills to fully engage in life, rather than cautiously and half-heartedly participating in life. Some part of us knows this, and that part will do its very best to get our attention if we are stubbornly hiding out of self-distrust and fear.

That internal reminder is one of the best gifts we have. It is the voice that will, against all odds, keep insisting that you shine your light. Have you ever stood by a horse with carrots in your pocket? The horse will keep nudging you, gently butting its head into your arm over and over until you finally produce the carrot for the clever creature to eat. The horse knows the carrot is there; the smell gives it away every time. Though you may try to ignore the sacred purpose in your life, hopefully your own internal objection will keep nudging you insistently. Your whole self knows that you have a purpose, and if you are lucky, it will keep nudging until you share it with yourself and the world.

Stop and reflect for a few minutes and notice how you think—which part of your brain seems more dominant? Do you like to gather facts and do research before you make a decision? Do you become exasperated when you think others spend too much time brain-storming—those people who increasingly like to think of more and more ways that things could be done? If you have answered yes to these or similar questions, you are likely to prefer left-brain thinking.

Or are you more inclined toward the other camp? Do you love to imagine possibilities? Do you tune into many ways of knowing things, only some of which come from traditional sources like books? Are you comfortable expressing emotions? If you answered yes to these and similar questions, consider yourself as having right-brain preferences. Try the Right or Left Activity that follows to check your preferences.

Activity: *Right or Left?*

Circle the statements that most reflect how you make decisions, and then put a check by any that sound appealing but you are not using much (yet). This will give you a sense of your general tendencies and possible additional preferences. For a more detailed report on your preferences, consider taking the Emergenetics® measure (described in the following section and in the Resources section at the back of the book).

Left Brain	Right Brain
like to research.	I prefer to use my imagination.
To feel comfortable, I want to understand the whole project and consider the context before I make a decision.	I enjoy using my intuition to make decisions. Even if all the facts are available, I probably won't read them.
I like to know the details.	I value my emotions and want to express them.
I prefer to get involved in situations in which I can be in control.	I consider what will happen to the people involved in making a decision.

Your brain dominance influences how you live your life. Your preferences guide you throughout the day as you choose to engage with one project or another, as you evaluate a problem, and even as you decide how to play or to exercise. We work best when we are able to integrate these skills. For example, the left side of the brain is usually the location of the main language center; it hears the words and puts them in context. The right side of the brain adds the emotional nuance. Without both of these messages together, we are in trouble. As Newberg, D'Aquili, and

Rause clarify, "Clearly, the generation of human conscious awareness, in all its multilayered fullness, depends upon the harmonious integration of both sides of the brain" (23).

Usually we can access both sides of our brain, but one way of thinking is likely to be more dominant. A habitual way of thinking that leaves out alternative perspectives may be the source of dissatisfaction for you.

EMERGENETICS®

Some of the people featured in the 2% in Motion stories have taken a thinking preference measure called an *Emergenetics*® profile. This profile presents information on four thinking and three behavioral preferences. Each thinking preference is associated with a color: It looks at two types of left-brain thinking—analytical (blue) and structural (green)—and two types of right-brain thinking—conceptual (yellow) and social (red). Another combination is presented as well—abstract thinkers, that is, folks with preferences in analytical (blue) and conceptual (yellow). Abstract thinkers like big picture thinking; they notice the forest more than the trees. On the other hand, concrete thinkers with preferences in structural (green) and social (red) thinking prefer to focus on the details and are much more likely to zero in on the trees than the forest. This measure also includes three behavior preferences that go hand-in-hand with the emotional intelligence skills we have been discussing: expressiveness, assertiveness, and flexibility and are seen on the outer ring of the pie. This system is powerfully explained by one of its creators, Geil Browning, in her book, *Emergenetics: Tap Into the New Science of Success* (2006). A sample from a profile can be found on the next page.

No one preference is superior to another. This personality measure is designed to help people know their own strengths and help them recognize that people think differently. Imagine having a research and development team that was composed entirely of people who had analytical and conceptual preferences, but that had no social (people-oriented) preferences. They might develop the most novel and cost-efficient products ever, like solar-heated coat hangers. But without the

EMERGENETICS®

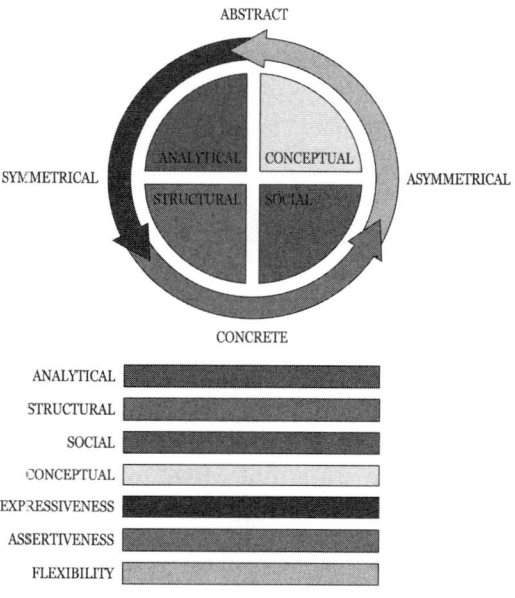

input from the people-pleasing social folks, they would be astonished when nobody ever bought a single one!

The thinking preferences are derived from brain dominance theory; the behavioral preferences relate to emotional intelligence behavioral awareness. The profiles reflect how much we prefer to think from the left-brain analytical and structural modes and how much we prefer to think from the conceptual and social modes of the right brain. Because of the association with the colors, most people remember their preferences easily and then start to have "ah-ha" insights into how their thinking is complemented by or different from those around them. The story of Theresa and Bill, which follows, shows how they used their preferences to move through conflict.

2% in Motion

TRUE COLORS

Theresa and Bill had been operating their design company for 10 years when they started working with an executive coach. The coach is helping them cope with the challenges of the current economy and improve the productivity of the business. They both took the EQi and the Emergenetics measure, and then they focused on understanding the present situation and setting development goals. Emergenetics helped them understand the different ways they think about the company and its challenges. Theresa is an abstract, analytical (blue) and conceptual (yellow) thinker. She looks for the big picture, wants the details so she can analyze the situation, and likes to make quick decisions. Bill, on the other hand, is a concrete, structural (green) and social (red) thinker. He prefers to pay attention to the people, move slowly, and organize carefully. When they can appreciate their differences, they are a strong team; when they can't, they can easily be frustrated by their different preferences.

Their understanding grew even richer as Theresa and Bill looked at how their emotional intelligence preferences matched up. Theresa found she has significant strengths in assertiveness and optimism; Bill's biggest strengths are empathy and interpersonal relationships. They learned to look at the whole picture of their strengths and weaknesses, both individually and as a team. Then they developed a strategically balanced game plan to use their strengths to address their weaknesses and thereby accomplish their goals. %

Use the following exercise as a way to explore different strategies for decision-making. Developing this kind of flexibility can be a valuable way to understand your preference, which is probably your strength. Just because one way of thinking is a strength, however, doesn't mean that you aren't, or can't become, great at solving a problem from a different perspective. Remember, choice is certainly better than no choice. You are likely to get much better solutions if you will experiment with alternative forms of solving a problem. This is particularly valuable to apply as a part of your approach in carrying out your 2% Project.

Activity: *Applying Different Thinking Preferences*

Scenario: The Host with "the Most"
You are hosting a large international conference of experts and leaders in the professional area most important to evolving your career. Of course, career development is only a part of the reason you care about doing a tremendous job. You also hold these people in high regard. They are providing important contributions to the field and are making the world a better place to live. You greatly respect these folks and want to show that respect and thank them properly. So here is the challenge:

How do you want to prepare for your three days together at the conference facility? What factors are most important to address in advance? What do you want to be sure you pay attention to during the conference?

Your mission, should you choose to accept it:

1. Choose to first prepare from just your right brain or your left brain perspective—the one you perceive to be your dominant style. Write a list of everything you can think of that will help you fully prepare and host the conference. Be thorough. If you are developing a left-brain list, you might begin with pens, paper, food, background information—now take it from here. If you are preparing a right-brain list, you might begin with fun gifts, acknowledgements for their accomplishments, planning of the breaks—now take it from here.

2. Get up, walk around, and get a glass of water, all the time letting go of your thinking about this exercise. When you return, clear your mind of the last way of thinking about it and consider the situation from the other perspective—either right or left brain—whichever you did not follow first.

3. Take a break again and let your focus relax. When you come back, approach the challenge by integrating your capabilities and thinking from both sides of your brain. In other words, integrate your two lists.

4. Review your three lists. What do you notice? Which way is best for you to approach this problem? Would it be the same for other problems? Your answer might be, "It depends." That is understandable, but then take it further. Under what circumstances are you better off considering a problem from a left-brain perspective? When is right brain better? When is a mixed perspective best?

5. You probably feel more comfortable working with challenges from one perspective than another. That is normal. However, there is great value in expanding your skills so that you are able to take another look at a matter of importance to you. Make some notes about how you want to strengthen your ability to think from both sides of your brain and how you want to be able to integrate that thinking. Note, perhaps in your 2% Journal, how you will use this to enhance your 2% Project.

THE BODY'S WISDOM

This chapter is all about learning how to tap into your body's many sources of wisdom. For instance, focus your attention on your solar plexus (just above your navel) and count the beats of your heart as you exhale slowly. This refocuses your attention away from the verbal chatter of the ego/mind. It centers your awareness on an internal rhythm, which makes it easier for your mind to be silent.

Where is this powerful subconscious, anyway, and how do you access it? Neuroscientist Candace Pert states it clearly: "Your body is your subconscious mind." In her tapes by the same title (2000), she describes the many ways our body is constantly teaching us. Listening to your body through reflective strategies and using kinesiology are two ways to tap into the wisdom source you walk around with every day. Chapter 4 includes several ideas for reflective strategies. Which ones have you tried? Which ones help you listen to your body? You can fold listening to this wisdom source into most reflective strategies. For example, if you write in a journal, try this one: have a conversation with your body or with a part that seems to be insistently seeking your attention. If your back is aching, listen to it. Write a conversation that might begin like this:

> Me: Hi, Back, how are you today?
> Back: Oh, hi, glad you asked. I ache.
> Me: Thanks for telling me. What is the ache about?
> Back: Huh, you're asking! Well, I need to stretch more; remember those exercises you do every once in awhile and then promise to do daily?
> Me: Yes, and I know I feel better when I stretch. Sorry I haven't done it more. What else?
> Back: Well, I feel burdened with the job of getting these big reports out. It seems like too much for me.
> Me: My back is stressed about the work? Well, it makes sense to me. I don't stretch you, and I do stress you. I haven't even thought about the projects much; just got to do what I have to do.
> Back: Well, it's hard for me.
> Me: I get it. I need to start paying better attention. I'll come back and write more another day. Now I need to go stretch!
> Back: I feel better already. Thanks!

That conversation may seem like a stretch to you, but this kind of communication actually occurs for some people. Maybe you won't get words, but you may see a color or hear a sound. If so, repeat that sound out loud or the color mentally as a way of saying "Roger, we copy that." This is already huge progress in learning to communicate with your subconscious mind. As it learns to trust you and believes you are listening and taking it seriously, you might be able to ask it how it wants to feel instead of the pain. If it is responsive to you, you might hear a different sound, see a different color, or sense words, such as rest, stretch, and love.

If you do hear a request from your subconscious mind, repeat that mentally in confirmation and do your best to remember it a hundred or a thousand times a day. Remembering the symbol of the desired state your body would prefer is likely to bring the new state into being if you persist with loving diligence.

Here's a second way of gaining information from your body.

> The most beautiful thing we can experience is the mysterious. It is the source of all true art and science.
>
> —Albert Einstein

Based on the use of kinesiology, it is known as muscle response testing. E. Whalen describes the four-step process to muscle testing in his Foreword to *Power vs. Force* (1995). It is quite simple: you extend one of your arms, and then someone asks you yes-or-no questions. Your arm will stay strong if the answer is yes and it will go down if the answer is no. If this seems a little questionable to you, review the research and try it. Of course, it is best if you can work with a person who has already used the process, so see if you can find a local kinesiologist. Many chiropractors also use this method. If you become comfortable with this process, you can use it to fine-tune your work with your 2% Project. If you feel like quitting on a part of the project, check it out. Is it something you need to see through, or would a new approach be better? Your body knows the answer.

Whalen continues his description:

> *What seems to be at work is a form of communal consciousness, spiritus mundi, or as Hawkins calls it, following Jung, a "database of consciousness." The phenomenon seen so commonly in other social animals—whereby a fish swimming at one edge of a school will turn instantaneously when its fellows a quarter mile away flee a predator—also pertain in some subconscious way to our species (5–6).*

Work with your subconscious to know what you know. You are probably in for some pleasant surprises.

2% in Motion

ON ALL CYLINDERS

At age 36, Marcus lost his good-paying job when the multinational computer company where he worked went through a downsizing. His job had been creative, and resplendent with job security. Until, suddenly, he wasn't safe at all—he was out of a job. Fortunately, Marcus had been seeking to understand himself better and this shock fast-forwarded the inquiry process. As he tried out different ways of thinking and took the Emergenetics measure, he found that he had a lot more preference for the big picture, brainstorming, conceptual way of thinking than he had realized. Yes, he had a strong preference for analytical thinking, but he had other strengths that he hadn't used much.

Marcus realized that now was his chance to try something new. But he wanted it to be a lasting contribution to the evolution of his whole life process, so he took time to evaluate and think things through as he chose his next career. He wrote in his journal, talked with respected peers, and hired a job coach. The result: Marcus realized that to be true to the call of his heart's longing, it was time to set up his own business. When I last heard from him, he said life was pretty frantic as the business was just getting going, so he wasn't sure his life was simpler, but he felt like he was thinking on all cylinders, and that excited him. %

APPLYING YOUR MAP AROUND THE WORLD

In *A Theory of Everything*, Ken Wilber includes the following quote from Bill Joy, the co-founder of Sun Microsystems: "Within 50 years, technological advances in genetics, robotics, and nanotechnology might mean the end of the human species." (2002, 104).

Wilber cautions us to take quite seriously Bill Joy's warning. Our ability to create material objects, such a nuclear bombs, has outpaced our universal consciousness. It is through strategies such as implementing our 2% Solution that we will evolve our thinking and our actions. These enhanced skills will help us make good decisions to contextualize and govern our technological acumen. Think of the 2% Solution as a way to integrate human and technical acumen.

Our personal maps of reality, even the tools we use to make maps, continually become outdated. So we need new maps, such as those offered by Spiral Dynamics integral and the All Quadrant/All Level (AQAL) viewpoint offered by Wilber.

ALL QUADRANT/ALL LEVEL APPROACH

In his seminal work *Sex, Ecology, Spirituality* (1995), Wilber undertook to integrate the apparent differences in the works of the world's great thinkers. He found that to fully view any interaction, it must be looked at from four perspectives: the individual, the collective, the objective, and the subjective. The following diagram, derived from Wilber's *A Theory of Everything* (2001, 43), demonstrates the perspectives.

I (self and consciousness)	IT (brain and organism)
WE (culture and worldview)	ITS (social system and environment)

Source: © Ken Wilber. Used with permission.

Place your 2% Project on this four-part grid and see how your bases are covered. Since your project will certainly be about you, the upper left "I" quadrant is no doubt included. Does part of your project account for how you interface with the social world and culture? Your answer is probably yes in some way, so the lower left "We" quadrant will be involved. This isn't a surprise, as this quadrant contains our interpersonal relationships. The upper right "IT" quadrant is where your body fits into the mix, for example, addressing its needs for exercise and nutrition. The lower right quadrant, ITS, addresses your relationships with political, economic, and technological systems and the environment. All these systems impact the way we live our lives, especially as globalization continues at an accelerating pace. Do they all fit your 2% Project? How about your life long 2% Solution?

Your 2% Solution can help you to more consciously participate in how these ways of organizing influence you and how you influence them. Is your 2% Solution about yourself? About society? Is it about further understanding the basic organisms you are working with (perhaps your office or your community), or is it complementing your community or office with systemic thinking? It's not necessary to have your project touch all four quadrants. Of course, your 2% Project should meet your particular needs. However, it's more likely your 2% Solution will embrace a bigger picture and may benefit from incorporating all four quadrants. Using the four quadrants helps us restructure our lives and move in ways that make us more inclusive. We more fully recognize which parts of the world are demanding our attention, and that helps us respond with clarified intention.

Engage Your EQ: *Problem Solving*

You can develop your own brilliant method of decision-making by integrating your process of analysis using your analytical and intuitive selves. Review the material we covered in this chapter on using your heart brain, your belly brain, and your analytical brain. Whether you are working on implementing your 2% Project, a key issue at work, or one of your passionate concerns in your community, whole-brain thinking will give you a more complete picture of what is happening than if you just use part of your database. This approach will lead you to comprehensive and lasting decisions.

Learning how to bring all the facts, considerations, and possibilities of any situation together and then deciding on an effective answer is no small skill. It requires integrating many streams of social, emotional, and factual information. Problem-solving is a skill you will want to draw on throughout the implementation of your 2% Project. And there is a bigger benefit: these skills will extrapolate to the rest of your life!

Most people use one of three quite different styles to solve problems—left-brain analytical, right-brain conceptual, or a hybrid. As you did with the earlier right brain / left brain activity, The Host with "the Most", experiment with different approaches. First follow your natural way of problem-solving, and do so thoroughly. Then tackle the problem again using another style and its strategies.

Thus, if you are mostly analytical in your approach, pay more attention to your dreams and spend quiet time just letting guidance come to you. If you're mostly right-brained in your approach, exercise the discipline to also gather the facts, write them down, and consider their relative merits. If your preference is in the middle, then sharpen your skills in both directions by paying even more attention. Whatever approach to problem-solving you use, it is a skill you will need to use throughout your 2% Project, and your results will be a direct reflection of your investment.

Key steps to good problem-solving are:

- Think things through before acting on big matters.

- Consider the consequences of actions and choices. If they don't support your goals, don't do them.

- Weigh different options.

- Connect the dots—note how decisions mutually influence one another. Synthesize and harmonize your actions so they support mutual goals for an integrated lifestyle. You can build your skills by playing strategy games or even dabbling with mind-benders.

A SENSE OF MEANING

You may have a sense of what is meaningful in your life, but where does that meaning come from? Is the source of true meaning physical, mental, emotional, or spiritual, or does it have components from all these categories? Living an inspired life requires connection with what is personally meaningful. Depending on the context of a situation, the inspiration may come through the physical (planting a tree to enjoy shade in the summer), mental (learning math because formulas are fun), emotional (noticing what feels good, and repeating it often, like giving and receiving hugs from loved ones), or spiritual (moving toward goals that hold us to a higher moral and creative standard and serve more than our own self-interests). Knowing where you find your sense of meaning is central to the success of your 2% Solution and your 2% Project.

Finding personal meaning gives us motivation. Where is the source of your motivation? Is it directly accessible to your everyday conscious mind, or does the burning awareness that you can do more lie deeper within, at a level that is much less conscious and much trickier to access? Find your motivation. I am talking about the awareness that has led you to read this book and to work with your 2% Solution.

TUNE IN YOUR MIND

- Embrace whole-mind thinking by taking the time to listen to your head, your heart, your belly, and your soul. Expand your skills in integrating these powerful sources of wisdom.

- Notice the difference between your own right- and left-brain ways of knowing the world. Understand your preferences and seek to identify those of others. Try to evaluate your options from several different points of view, not just your usual approach.

- Welcome the information coming from both your conscious and your unconscious awareness of the world. Listen to your body; it too can be a teacher.

- Use these skills to understand and express your emotions and to fully solve problems that come your way.

TUNE OUT THE NOISE

- Do not get caught in the habit of looking at an issue in just one way. Take time to look for surprising and different viewpoints.

- Avoid ignoring all the signals you are receiving from your body. If it is giving you a message, be it pain or joy, there is a reason. Pay attention.

A SNEAK PREVIEW

Besides chocolate and a great skiing or beach vacation, what do you really truly want? Chapter 9 explores how to apply the 2% Process to your life at work. Leaders will show you how to bring your 2% wisdom to work. Learn how to improve your stress management skills as a key component of EQ.

9/

THE AUTHENTIC LEADER
Your 2% Solution at Work

Sam is a founding partner and CEO of a successful advertising firm in the Midwest. One of his defining traits is his creativity. He can turn a hopelessly ordinary situation into a memorable and moving event. It's what makes his blood flow and gets him excited when he gets up in the morning. The ideas come at lightning speed; maybe that's why he's in constant motion. There was a time when he buzzed in and out, leaving a trail of possibilities behind him, showing his staff how to think out of the box and on the fly. They loved him. Ironically, the more successful Sam's firm became, the more his time was taken up with administrative functions. He nagged his staff. They grumbled. He grumbled and watched his joy ebb away and his energy dwindle.

He looked for random ways to infuse happiness back into his job. What he didn't immediately recognize was how far from his center he had drifted. He found his way to a 2% seminar and discovered the path back to his Esprit d'Core. Through his 2% Project, Sam sought his staff's help to figure out why work wasn't working for him. His creativity is apparent in his approach to his project. He's not the kind of guy to retreat and write; he can't sit still long enough. Naturally, Sam came up with a novel idea about how to get back to his center.

He engaged his staff to help. Sam took them on a field trip—to the swing set in Sam's neighborhood. They filmed him there as he talked about the inspiration that makes his creative juices flow and his inherent need to be creative. They went to other significant places that mattered to him—his conference room, his office, his art studio, and his favorite park. He made a powerful video that renewed his passion and clarified what it is he loves about his work. His staff was thrilled when Sam handed over the administrative details and plunged back into what he does best and what he's passionate about—his creative skills to solve problems. He also dusted off his kiln, fired it up, and got back to making pottery. %

Many of us go through our work lives longing to be more fulfilled, aligned with our passions, and emotionally in tune. These feelings bring joy to our efforts, yet we don't often know how to make them a reality. By now you've discovered that the 2% Solution incorporates proven techniques and can bring important benefits to the workplace, increasing both productivity and job satisfaction. A 2% Project is flexible enough to adapt to changing needs and circumstances within the workplace and in private life. In this chapter you will learn how to:

- Draw on your 2% Solution to improve your leadership and workplace performance.

- Leverage Pareto's 80/20 Rule for greater results with only 2% of your time.

- Transform the values of your 2% Process into behaviors that consistently support your accountability and ethical behavior at work.

- Inspire others through your personal influence as a servant leader.

- Manage your stress so you survive and thrive.

Whether by necessity or passion, most of us dedicate a significant amount of time to work. No matter what your focus is for your 2%

Solution, if it is truly targeted on the core meanings for your life, it will similarly bring deeper meaning to your work. The universal themes that the 2% Solution is designed to address can make a world of difference for you in the workplace. Imagine that your work life is characterized by acting authentically, operating from your strengths, connecting with your core wisdom and your heart's desire, and bringing it all to life. Sounds like a great job! It can be yours; it's not a fantasy. Even when the inevitable chaos happens, the momentum from living purposefully will keep you grounded in your center.

THE PARETO PRINCIPLE, REDEFINED

In the late 1800s and the beginning of the last century, Italian economist Vilfredo Pareto created a system of economic, social, and political thought that still warrants our serious consideration. His 80/20 Rule has infiltrated the worlds of management and strategic development, providing influential guidance on how to prioritize effectively. It resides at the heart of why we focus on our strengths, and ultimately highlights the salience of the 2% Solution. The 80/20 Rule has been incorporated by successful businesses and professionals for nearly a century. Now you can refine it even further.

In essence, the 80/20 Rule refers to the principle that 20 percent of our actions produce most of the beneficial effects we enjoy. Thus, the most productive 20 percent are considered the vital few and the other 80 percent the trivial. In an organization, 20 percent of the top performers are likely to deliver 80 percent of the results. Likewise, 80 percent of the mistakes or troublesome matters are likely to come from 20 percent of your employees, clients, or widgets.

This theory began with Pareto and has been augmented over time. In 1998, Richard Koch wrote *The 80/20 Principle: The Secret to Success by Achieving More with Less*, in which he emphasizes the importance of prioritizing. Tom Butler-Bowdon, in his *50 Self-Help Classics*, choose Koch's book as one of the 50 best all-time books, because applying this principle leads to truly effective action in a world cluttered with the trivial. Butler-Bowdon wrote that "80/20 thinking is the combination of ambition with a relaxed and confident manner. It involves reflective thinking (allowing insights to come, rather than leaping into action), unconventional use of time and a hedonistic philosophy" (2003, 185).

Again, Pareto's famous rule is that 80 percent of the value comes from 20 percent of the items, 80 percent of the creativity is produced by 20 percent of the team, 80 percent of the problems come from 20 percent of the students, and so on. My research shows something even more amazing. More dramatic results can be achieved when that focus is narrowed from 20 percent to 2 percent. Wise application of your 2% Solution can distill your high payoff priorities down to your *highest* payoff priority, letting you experience exponentially increased results.

My decades of experience as an attorney, a therapist, and now a consultant have convinced me that every person seeks to contribute meaningfully in life and, quite simply, to be happy. In fact, the two are inextricably linked. And when these goals are integrated through a genuine 2% Solution, you're spot on! Life works with a newfound harmony, as if an alchemical intervention has occurred. That isn't to promise you won't have hard times—we all do—but you'll have a vastly expanded set of resources to deal with those challenges, resources that will also enhance your enjoyment of the fortunate events in life.

Deep truths find congruence with one another. The 2% Process calls for even more radical prioritizing than the 80/20 Rule and maximizes effectiveness through reflective thinking and unconventional use of time, and by finding our deepest level of happiness. No amount of chocolate, gourmet dining, or any other hedonistic pleasure brings real meaning—pleasure, certainly, but not meaning. Meaning comes from the sustainable engagement with the natural world and all our human allies. By moving beyond the pursuit of pleasure to the search for higher meaning and

> While we have the gift of life, it seems to me the only tragedy is to allow part of us to die, whether it is our spirit, our creativity, or our glorious uniqueness.
>
> —Gilda Radner

deeper connectedness, you are able to gain the increased benefit from much less of your time—2 percent instead of 20 percent. The key point is to move away from the trivial concerns of the ego and toward that which truly matters to your heart, soul, and spirit.

....

MOTIVATE YOURSELF

Implementing your 2% Project and expressing it so well that can you influence others requires motivation. The more you learn about yourself and how to bring out the best in yourself, the better your life works. Use your powers of reflection and reality testing to notice what causes your soul to sing. Assess the circumstances that allow you to do your best work and take note of those that bring lesser results. The more you know about yourself, the more effectively you can take personal responsibility for your life. No one else can, or ever will, lead the good life for you.

Research shows workers are motivated by the ability to be creative, by praise and recognition, and by purposeful engagement. Yet organizations are often weak in providing support for these core criteria. A 2004 Gallup poll showed that 65 percent of workers in the United States received no praise or recognition in the workplace in the last year. The U.S. Department of Labor reports that the primary reason people leave organizations is that they don't feel appreciated. These are dismal statistics, and they are especially frustrating because they are so unnecessary. You can make a difference for yourself and for those you manage and otherwise influence in the workplace.

When you enter the workplace, your voice doesn't need to be silenced. However, you do have to take responsibility for your own motivation and happiness. Too many managers and leaders still have no idea what their workers really need or how to provide it. Your personal happiness is not contingent upon whether your manager is able to discern what you need. Great managers do a better job of figuring that out, but ultimately, it's up to you to know what you need and to make the changes to get it. Sometimes that translates into a job change, but often it can be job or attitude tweaks. Remember that your attitude is exclusively within your power. Furthermore, there are many managers who would be delighted to meet your needs if you only told them.

Through my work at Collaborative Growth, I continuously focus on enhancing leadership and management skills of my clients. Therefore, I agree that leadership has a major responsibility, but you must always consciously acknowledge and celebrate that the true point of power is within yourself. Take your job, and especially your attitude at work, and shape it any way you want! Don't abdicate your power and authority by waiting for your boss to become enlightened on how to establish a motivating and creative environment. Bring in your own motivation, notice what makes you creative, and find ways, even if they are little ones, to build them into your work world.

Activity: *The Choice Is All Yours*

1. On a scale of 1 to 10, how motivated are you now on a typical day at work? ___

2. Why?

3. On the same scale, how motivated are you to do your 2% Solution and other activities that you love? ___

4. Why?

5. What's different? How can you bring your most positive motivators to your work and to other important parts of your life? This is a very significant question, so take some time to consider it. Go to a quiet place where you can reflect and think creatively, or find a way to talk about it. Doing more of what works well for you is guaranteed to expand your happiness. Once you are ready, make some notes.

HOW IMPORTANT IS CREATIVITY, ANYWAY?

In today's highly competitive world of work, a key ingredient for individual development and organizational survival is the ability to be creative. It is central to your exuding the positive influence you have to offer. This creativity is at the root of better widgets, improved production and distribution systems, innovation of every kind, and enhanced connections with employees and others. Creativity is generally described as the ability to produce something new, which will enhance the beauty and quality of life. In the workplace, that usually translates into new products, services, and better productivity. It may also come in the form of developing improved relationships or enhancing motivation, finding a way to cut costs, or producing a runaway bestseller.

We learned of Sam's yearning for creativity at the beginning of this chapter. He developed his own creative way to restore that essential ingredient in his life. Like Sam, you also need outlets for expressing your creativity—the workplace should be one of them, in addition to ways of expressing it in your hobbies as well as your family and community relationships. Being creative is the expression of a natural gift you have, but if you don't nourish it, your creativity will wither on the vine as your neuronal pathways begin to turn into ruts. You can revitalize it, but it's always better to continuously nourish this vibrant and unique part of you.

> Creativity is a central source of meaning in our lives...[and] when we are involved in it, we feel that we are living more fully than during the rest of life.
>
> —Mihaly Csikszentmihalyi, author of *Flow*

Teresa Amabile, a professor at the Harvard Business School, conducted years of research on creativity in the workplace. Amabile found that we are *not* induced to be more creative because of pay, an urgent deadline, or expected performance evaluations. Creativity results from intrinsic motivation. Potier interviewed her in the February 10, 2005 online issue of the *Harvard University Gazette* that "positive feelings—joy, love—are positively related to creativity, and the negative emotions—anger, fear, sadness—are negatively related to day-by-day creativity."

Creativity is something that comes from the inside out. A creative culture can be nourished by management and expanded by your willingness and positive intent. It will be hard for you to be happy, motivated, and influential at work if you don't feel creative in some way. However, you can trip yourself up by the way you describe creativity. A bus driver who helps people feel good when they board his or her bus is sharing creativity every time that help is offered. Think about how you can be creative at work. Do you

———————O———————

Who you are speaks so loudly I can't hear what you're saying.

—Ralph Waldo Emerson

———————O———————

need to expand the boundaries of your creativity? Next week find a new way to do a routine task at work that makes it more enjoyable. When you're done, celebrate your intention and your effort—regardless of the results! This will begin to teach your subconscious mind to look for opportunities to innovate.

WORKER, KNOW THYSELF

Whether you think of yourself at work as a CEO, leader, manager, or employee, the more you understand yourself—how you think, how you learn, your values, what sparks your curiosity—the more successful and influential you will be.

The *Harvard Business Review* published a special issue on managing yourself in January 2005. Peter Drucker's article on "Managing Oneself" emphasizes many of the points I have listed as critical to the success of your 2% Solution. Drucker has been a major force as a writer, consultant, and educator in the field of business management and development for over 30 years. He coined the term "knowledge worker" in the 70s to describe the change happening in the workplace for so many workers. In essence, a knowledge worker is a problem solver rather than a production worker and uses intellectual rather than manual skills at work.

If you are a knowledge worker, you use knowledge and information to add value, context, and detail to other streams of knowledge and information. A few examples of the many folks who fall in this category include people who work in IT, law, financial services, publishing, and health care. If you are a knowledge worker, you are likely to be even more responsible for managing your career than if you are a production worker. However, I have worked with people at factories, be they breweries or electrical products, and seen them face the same challenges. Drucker's sage advice begins with one I've emphasized throughout the book which is to focus on using and growing your strengths. He chides us to not act with "intellectual arrogance" by treating those who think or act differently as though they are inferior. Finally, he emphasizes we must continue to address bad habits instead of accepting them as a given.

Drucker has it right when he insists that the only way to find and build your strengths is through feedback; it's what I call reflection. He provides fascinating history on feedback analysis which he reports began in the fourteenth century and was later applied with rigor by John Calvin and Ignatius of Loyola. Drucker's analysis is that "the steadfast focus on performance and results that this habit produces explains why the institutions these two men founded, the Calvinist church and the Jesuit order, came to dominate Europe within 30 years" (102).

Just as I have emphasized throughout this book, Drucker urges that you understand how you learn and the styles that others use. Take advantage of the rich resources available by using tools within your organization such as the Myers-Briggs Temperament Indicator, Emergenetics, or go deeper with emotional intelligence measures such as the EQi or the EQ-360 so that you and your team have the ability to understand how one another learns, thinks, and behaves. To persuade someone, you need to speak his or her language; to do that, you need to understand how you learn and think, and how the other person learns and thinks. Then be willing to listen and engage them by using his or her style.

2% in Motion

WE ALL NEED SOMEBODY TO LEAN ON

Dennis is now beginning to brainstorm about creating his next 2% Project. He's a leader in a large training organization and is one of the most creative individuals I've ever met. Dennis enjoys considering big picture possibilities and then strategically connecting the resources and people to bring it into reality. He believes his next 2% Project will be to create a legacy for himself through discovering in what capacity he can best serve his fellow human beings. At the moment, he's thinking it might be around victim advocacy.

Dennis's story is included here because he is a perceptive leader, and he understands the potential as well as the challenges that surround the 2% Process. He conducted his first 2% Project in a leadership group as an assignment, and didn't get as much out of it as he now knows was possible. Your 2% Solution has to come from within you; neither you nor someone else can effectively force it. He felt forced because it was a group assignment. Furthermore, he cautions that each of us must have the right support around us when we address changing some pivotal part of our life. He has seen colleagues attempt to implement a 2% Project or similar process in order to change the direction of their life. However, when they didn't get support from their leaders they backed away. They opted not to take the challenge on, and in some cases that negatively impacted their self-confidence. %

As I have emphasized, if you are tackling difficult matters such as childhood issues, depression, or addiction, you need appropriate professional assistance. If you are a part of a leadership group, the leaders or peers in your work group should be sincerely committed to knowing and understanding you, and the meaning and scope of the challenge you are undertaking. Some take on projects with transformative potential, which initially proves to be more threatening and difficult than they first anticipated. When that happens, it is important to get support that brings more depth and experience to your corner.

If you are in a leadership group, a mentoring circle, or an ad hoc support group of friends and colleagues, pay attention to your support process, the timing, and your commitment to one another. If you are working on your 2% Project independently, remember that Step 8 calls for you to seek feedback from meaningful people in your life—mentors and others you respect. We don't live in this world alone. We need one another, and for you to negotiate a life-changing decision, you will always be better served if you are receiving knowledgeable and meaningful feedback from others who care about you. And then again, there are times when we know we must choose and act with no other support than the song that we hear from within us.

PREVENT SYSTEM SHUTDOWN

As discussed in Chapter 8, we have several brains, and every one of them is overloaded! Our bodies are burdened and our brains are over-taxed. Psychiatrist Edward Hallowell has taken his extensive work with Attention Deficit Disorder (ADD) and applied it to identify a new neu-rological event, Attention Deficit Trait (ADT). Hallowell wrote in "Why Smart People Underperform," Harvard Business Review (2005) that this disorder is the result of our brains being asked to process enormous amounts of data. "As our minds fill with noise—feckless synaptic events signifying nothing—the brain gradually loses its capacity to attend ful-ly and thoroughly to anything" (56). He continues that we are blessed with a large cortex, yet we put enormous pressure on the frontal lobes, which is where we do the processing referred to as executive function-ing. In other words, there is an environmental (behavioral) fix for this disorder, which is caused by our fast-paced world. Hallowell goes on to suggest several cures, including:

- Promote positive emotions. Emotion is the on/off switch for executive functioning.

- Comfortably connect with a colleague. The deep centers of the brain send messages through the pleasure center to the area that assigns resources to the frontal lobes. This sense of human connection causes executive functioning to hum. Make time at least every four to six hours for a "human moment," a face-to-face exchange with a person you like.

- Take physical care of your brain. Sleep, eat a good diet, and exercise. Organize by breaking large tasks into smaller ones and keeping a section of your work space clear.

Many of these recommendations are familiar. We read and hear re-peatedly to get exercise and enough sleep. What is particularly helpful is that he has pulled these points together by helping us understand the impact on the brain—thus on our thinking and our behavior—if we do let our brain get overloaded. Best of all, he provides doable guidelines for preventing overload and staying resourceful.

Engaging in the 2% Process can change your way of thinking. Instead of "doing what you've always done and getting what you've always gotten," it can lead you to develop the habits of being insightful and consistently acting on behalf of your own quality of life. Thus you can ultimately think and live beyond the oppression of routine—your own or others.

RECLAIM YOUR LIFE!

A shift is happening in the workplace—and this one is for the good of workers. People are voting against being a dead fish or using their effort to swim upstream. They want time and energy to swim with the kids or friends instead. Many are saying, "Okay, I'm going to manage for lifestyle and not just professional achievement." This is part of bringing balance into life—one of the most significant parts of the 2% Process, and it is happening in several creative ways. Some are being offered alternative work hours,

> A dead fish can float downstream, but it takes a live fish to swim upstream.
>
> —W. C. Fields

so they work ten hours for four days a week, or nine-hour days and receive every other Friday off; others downscale work and pay and modify their lifestyle accordingly. I am finding people of every generation increasingly taking advantage of these options—or demanding them.

There are many reasons for this shift. Some are attributed to the impact in the United States of 9/11, when many workers were awakened to the impermanence of life and made a commitment to live differently. For others it could be any number of factors—getting clear about their values, a health challenge, death of a loved one, or just getting plain fed up with the absurdity of overworking.

What is important about this trend is that people are reclaiming their lives. This is vital because no one else is likely to save us. We have to take personal responsibility for our lives. Your 2% Solution can be one of your very best learning opportunities for deciding to take charge of your life. Transformative opportunities are funny that way; when one step works well, it can lead you to take responsibility for other parts of your life as well. I'm certainly not suggesting you simply cut back your work hours, your responsibilities, or anything else. I am suggesting that you manage your career and your life so that you create time and space for that which you value most. No change has to be drastic. Simply note what is happening by meaningfully guiding 2% of your time, and then let the natural flow of the reflective wisdom you are gaining help you know if and when it's time to make other changes.

Activity: *All Dressed Up and Ready to Work*

Now is a good time to synthesize these ideas, because the point is to apply it to your own life. Give yourself the gift of some reflecting time, consider these questions, and jot some notes for yourself or write in your 2% Journal.

1. How are my relationships at work? Do I have face-to-face time regularly with people I enjoy?

2. Am I meaningfully engaged at work?

3. Do I feel like I'm drowning with thinking overload? If so, how often does it happen? To maintain my equilibrium I will... (make a list of what you'll do).

4. Am I working the best amount of hours given the needs required to live a balanced lifestyle? If not, what can I change? Feel free to think outside the box; after all, it is your life!

5. Am I taking charge of my career?

6. Am I expanding my strengths?

. . . .

POWERFUL 2% = POWERFUL LEADERSHIP

My suspicion is that you are more of a leader than you realize. We all deeply influence one another; it's the degree and nature of the influence that makes the crucial difference. While we explore this topic, take note of the roles in which you are an influencer.

Leadership is an art, and when it is done well, it inspires confidence and commitment in others. The critical need for finding top-notch leadership is demonstrated by the thousands of books and classes on the topic. It is one of the hottest topics we address at Collaborative Growth. Why all the interest? Why the need for all the books, classes, and coaching on how to become an effective leader?

While our world needs leaders, the *type* of leadership is the critical question. Servant leadership, a concept expounded by Robert Greenleaf in his book *The Servant-Leader Within* (2003), is deeply congruent with the exercise of the meaningful life the 2% Solution calls for. It's the form which naturally happens as you develop authentic creativity and motivation. When you exhibit these characteristics, you are a leader no matter what your title at work.

Greenleaf defines servant leadership as follows:

> The servant-leader is servant first...It begins with the natural feeling that one wants to serve, to serve first. Then conscious choice brings one to aspire to lead. He or she is sharply different from the person who is leader first, perhaps because of the need to assuage an unusual power drive or to acquire material possessions. For such it will be a later choice to serve—after leadership is established. The leader-first and the servant-first are two extreme types. Between them there are shadings and blends that are part of the infinite variety of human nature (www.greenleaf.org).

A DEFINING MOMENT

The key to successful leadership today is influence, not authority, and that happens by walking your talk, being a great role model.

Servant leaderships, then, is another means for following through on your true purpose while influencing others in the process. Throughout this book I have pointed out ways to develop behavior that is congruent with whom you really are. The authenticity at the heart of all inspiring leadership comes from the leader's connection with his or her core purpose. The message and the capabilities that activate it cannot be faked. Leadership is demonstrated through consistent attitudes, beliefs, and nonverbal communication more than through specific words or policies. It is full development as a whole person—heart, mind, and soul— that is the trademark of a great leader. And this is precisely the purpose of the 2% Solution. By knowing and acting in accordance with your deepest wisdom, you will develop a highly respected stature that acts as a magnet to others. This is the stuff of natural, authentic leadership.

GREAT LEADERS CREATE MEANING

One of the most frequent laments I hear these days is that our world needs more honest, intelligent leaders. Well, here is an admonition to a higher level of responsibility: Be the change that's needed! Most people will never be a president or prime minister, but as long as you consistently show that you are honest, have integrity, and reflect the meaningful connection that you have found in your life, you will be an effective leader.

Margaret Wheatley, the well-known author of *Science and the New Leadership* (1992), is a bright voice in explaining the new demands on organizational leadership. She combines the principles of quantum theory, quark physics, and chaos in a user-friendly way to help us respond effectively to change and chaos in the increasingly complex world we share. She joins our 2% chorus in singing the praises and the necessity of creating meaning. She writes (135):

> *I have also seen companies make deliberate use of meaning to move through times of traumatic change. . . .all of us want so much to know the "why" of what is going on. (How often have you heard yourself or others say, "I just wish they would tell me why we're doing this.") We instinctively reach out to leaders who work with us on creating meaning. Those who give voice and form to our search for meaning, and who help us make our work purposeful, are leaders we cherish, and to whom we return gift for gift.*

We need meaning in our organizational lives just as much as in our personal lives, so take the skills and knowledge you are learning from your 2% Process to work. It will help you sing your song, and you'll be a role model for others to sing theirs as well. Your example will provide them the invitation to find the meaning and purpose in their lives.

··

THE EMOTIONALLY INTELLIGENT CEO

The dollar and the people value of applying emotional intelligence in the workplace is well documented by research. Earlier, we discussed the benefits of working with EQ measures, such as the EQi. Part of the value is that we can work with the key individuals and identify the profile of skills which distinguish those who are most successful in their profession. For example, the EQi has been used with corporate leaders such as the Young Presidents' Organization (YPO), Young Entrepreneurs' Organization (YEO), and at the Center for Creative Leadership (CCL). Steven Stein, CEO of Multi-Health Systems, the distributor of several EI measures, reports that "direct connections have been found between emotional intelligence and leadership in all of these groups" (2002). In one research study, Stein reported a difference found among CEOs in Ontario, Canada. They have higher total EQ scores and higher skills in independence, assertiveness, optimism, self-actualization, and self-regard than normally found.

In short, your openness, connection to meaning, and emotional and social intelligence skills are all vital parts of your competency as a leader. Your 2% Solution can be focused to help you expand any of these skills.

2% in Motion

BECOMING AN AUTHENTIC LEADER
Dede, a vice president with a financial institution, had been there years and was quite successful. Springing from early childhood

traumas, being perfect was critical to Dede. She dressed well, spoke well, and got her work done on time—who could ask for more? Well, Dede's spirit asked for more. The calling knocking on her inner door was for her to become more accepting of people— all people, not just those who looked and acted like her.

Dede's mother had been institutionalized for mental illness for a year when Dede was in third grade. Her father had worked hard and kept the family together, but Dede emerged from childhood afraid to show people the fears and uncertainties behind her perfect veneer. She became an evangelical Christian and felt she was opening her heart to others by tolerating those who were different.

Dede's 2% Solution broke that shield wide open. She wrote that she wanted to be a more authentic leader in her community. She wanted to reach out to the community to satisfy personal and professional goals and make a difference in the lives of others. To do this, Dede recognized that she needed to overcome many long-held prejudices. She took on the inspiring intention of loving all humankind.

She worked through her leadership group, studied Reiki and began practicing it, volunteered with the Visiting Nurse Association, and reflected on her life extensively, by herself and with trusted role models. Slowly, she began to move beyond the evangelical stage of her faith, as she described it, so now it is "clearer, less cluttered, and truer." Dede continued, "It slowly came to me that if I really wanted to know life, I couldn't contribute and give while at the same time condemning a portion of the population. Before I shed that stuff, the compassion I have today would never have been possible."

Dede's leadership capabilities were concretely enhanced by her 2% Solution. For example, when she chaired the United Way drive, her new attitude and enthusiasm caused her to set a high goal and the organization exceeded it by 18 percent. Dede exclaims that "the synergy of being involved with others is beneficial to both them and me!"

Earlier in the book I have referred to the clarity provided by Stephen Covey in his *7 Habits of Highly Effective People*. His release of the next step, *The 8th Habit* (2004), is an excellent complement to the 2% Solution. Developing a 2% Solution is a powerful strategy for implementing his 8th step: to find your voice and inspire others to find theirs. Like the Collaborative Growth approach, Covey also emphasizes the importance of working with four intelligences—mind, body, heart, and spirit. Good ideas and strategies are strengthened by finding complementary paths. This resonates well with the 2% Solution work we are doing to create a meaningful engagement with life by being a whole person while thinking and acting with our whole mind—heart, brain, gut, and soul.

Engage Your EQ: *Stress Management*

Many of us feel that the stress in our lives is escalating at an absurd pace. I imagine that your 2% Solution is designed to help you work effectively with that stress factor. If you feel you are spending all your time stringing and unstringing your instrument and not singing your song, you are likely to feel stress—the stress of routines and underachievement, of not being satisfied with your life.

If you were to make a list of what you are coping with that has stressful impacts, you would need to look at all the parts of your life. Your list needs to address the daily impacts of money, transportation, and household management as well as the more high-profile issues of a new you, your significant other, or a health issue.

Interestingly, stress is not "bad"; it is just an event. Human beings actually need a healthy amount of stress to be motivated to act. Without sufficient amounts of stress, we are likely to be too laid back and under perform. With too much stress, performance again suffers.

Some of the people I interviewed about their 2% Projects indicated that their project initially brought more stress and less balance in their lives. However, the universal evaluation was that the cost was worth the payoff, because the project caused them to reorient their lives to be much more in sync with their values and ultimately reduced their stress. It is not about avoiding stress, but about managing how much we have and matching the stress with good resources.

One of the most effective stress management strategies ever is to get more exercise. This gets more oxygen into the bloodstream, speeding the pace with which toxins from stress are eliminated. Exercise also releases endorphins, which are hormones that enhance a feeling of well-being. Stress affects our body and our mind—the way we think, feel, and act. It can accumulate. Remember, too, that the stress of an event is determined by the amount of change it implies, not necessarily whether the change will be beneficial or detrimental. Marriage, birth, and voluntary job changes can be just as stressful as divorce and deaths.

Growing your EQ skills in managing stress

- First, recognize that stress is the *perception* of a threat and our reaction to that perception, then, second, manage your perception and reactions.

- When you encounter stress, *stop* before your thoughts escalate into the worst possible scenario. Simply saying "stop" can break the autonomic response and interrupt the negative stress cycle.

- After you stop, *breathe* deeply and release physical tension—the breath can help elicit the physiology of a relaxation response and divert you briefly from the stress.

- *Notice* where you are holding the stress in your body and let it go. Feel the relief with the relaxation.

- *Reflect* and focus your energy on the challenge at hand.

- *Choose* your response.

Other stress reducers:

- Exercise—even walking for just 10 minutes.

- Do something nice for yourself—go to a movie.

- Talk with a friend.

One of the four benefits of the 2% Solution, as we learned before, is congruency. When you align your values with your daily living, you produce true internal accountability, which is the integrity that arises out of deep and honest personal reflection. That reflection doesn't have to take a lot of time, but it does have to be honest. The honesty, which you practice as you implement your 2% Project, will make you both a better leader and a better employee. When you are congruent with your core truth, you are naturally accountable, because there aren't things you are denying or uncomfortable things from which you may be trying to hide. This fundamental commitment creates a naturally ethical engagement with the world. When you look in the mirror, you will feel comfortable with who you are and your choices.

TUNE IN YOUR MIND

- Move beyond Pareto's 80/20 Rule by achieving greater results with only 2% of your time.

- You are the one in charge of motivating yourself at work; manage your career for the success you value.

- Take time to connect with people you care about regularly and to create a supportive environment so your brain—in fact, your whole self—can function well.

- Take your 2% Solution to work. Your positive strategies will spill over to make you a positive influence in the workplace.

- Be proactive: take charge of your stress!

TUNE OUT THE NOISE

- Avoid brain strain; remember to breathe, interact, and religiously make time to connect with others.

- Avoid being isolated at work and at home. Especially look for ways to have face-to-face connections.

- All stress and no play makes Jack and Jill dull and uncreative. Don't forget to pay attention to your stress load.

A SNEAK PREVIEW

Being a whole person means integrating body, mind, heart, and soul. Keeping your soul alive may take different forms. Chapter 10 will help you discover that your recipe for wholeness could include adding religious or spiritual commitment, gardening, tai chi, and so much more.

10/

SING FROM YOUR SPIRIT
The Key to Self-Actualization

Meet John. He's a brilliant scientist—the real deal. He has a whiteboard covered with so many scribbled formulas and equations that there is barely a hint of white left on that board. John is the chief scientist for a major manufacturing company, and he is widely respected for having been responsible for engineering the chemistry of glass as a part of manufacturing industrial goods. It's a big thing.

Fast forward a few years. John is wrapping up a leadership development program that includes a 2% Project. His high-speed, left-brain, highly scientific mind makes a stunning realization: Having spent most of his adult life in the pursuit of scientific inquiry, he is suddenly curious about what it would be like to use the other part of his brain in the pursuit of spiritual inquiry. John decides to use his 2% Project to undertake an experiment centered on spirituality. (Leave it to a scientist to design a spirituality experiment to engage other parts of his brain and gain new insight about his own spirituality.)

Serendipitously, John is offered a retirement package and he chuckles as he factors that into his experiment and accepts the offer. Now five years into implementing his 2% Solution and happily retired, John is daily becoming a new man. John writes, "I simply am not the same person that I was then—I have been on a helter-skelter, not-at-all-organized rocket experience of growth. This is very important." He *has been receptive to his right brain capabilities of brainstorming and developing social connections, and he is volunteering with a children's group in Kenya and rebuilding homes in Honduras.* %

Developing our spiritual or religious nature is critical to countless adults who seek deeper meaning and resolution. Not surprisingly, many use the 2% Process to address this longing—for example, some choose to develop a path of meditation, participate in a religious group, play the piano for religious services, review their children's Sunday school lessons with them, practice tai chi, or follow a 12-Step Program. More important than the "what" is the focus and honesty with which the project is undertaken as searchers integrate body, mind, heart, and soul.

In this chapter you will:

- Check out "roads that diverge in a yellow wood"—is a religious, spiritual, agnostic, or atheistic path valuable for your 2% Process?

- Take a pilgrimage to gather wisdom from models for bringing the whole person—body and soul—to work.

- Learn by example by considering some 2% Projects that have implemented spiritual or religious strategies.

- Bring it all together through cross-training designed to promote living from the four domains of self: body, mind, heart, and soul.

- Expand your motivation and success through your EQ skills in self-actualization.

When your soul is in the dark, life is just a routine chess game. When your soul is on fire, life is a calling! It leads you to your Esprit d'Core, singing your song, and living with passionate equilibrium.

When I was a child, I kept waiting for a calling to be a member of a religious order. When that didn't happen, I thought I'd waited in vain; now I realize *this* work is my calling. It is humbling to share the wisdom I've gained from decades of asking, praying, probing, and learning to be patient. My evolving spirituality is my highest priority, and it sets the stage for all my work and play. I am honored whenever I have the opportunity to share some of what I've gained to help others make meaningful changes—so they can begin living even more fulfilling lives.

YOUR WAY TO TRUTH

You may consider yourself religious, spiritual, agnostic, or atheistic. The important question is, are seeking the deepest truths that will guide you to be your highest self? Are you seeking to understand the mysteries of your life, to find its deeper meaning, and to allow the wisdom that you gain to guide the direction of your search? If your answer is "Yes," I applaud you for finding the bearing that your soul wants to follow, and encourage you to tap into different strategies that may help you move in that direction.

This chapter will describe spiritual and religious methods that seekers have used to deepen their path. None of these examples are meant to reflect that one way is better than another. You must do the work to determine your own path; my hope is that these examples will help.

A DEFINING MOMENT

The term *spirituality* is used here to reflect a more comprehensive search for deeper meaning that may or may not include traditional religious practices, along with highly personal efforts to experience what transcends our mundane practical concerns. It includes following a spiritual path that leads beyond oneself to the greater power or source of life, reaching for a full communal meaning of greater good at all levels of higher truth.

LIFELONG BENEFITS OF 2%

Finding the path that gives your life its ultimate meaning is a journey, an ever-unfolding spiral. The deeper you go, the richer the meaning. The entire 2% Solution and the energy you put into your 2% Proj-

ect is geared toward a singular purpose: connecting with and expressing your core meaning. In turn, that is all about walking the path that
brings your true self—and all your particular gifts—to life. If your 2%
Solution is calling you to align
more deeply with your sense of the
divine, nothing will substitute for
the disciplined work of patiently
listening, uncovering, and giving
voice to your soul.

In the Gospel of Thomas, Jesus
says, "If you bring forth what is
within you, what you bring forth will
save you. If you do not bring forth
what is within you, what you do not
bring forth will destroy you."

Your 2% Solution is a way to
follow this profound directive. Notice in this quote that Jesus didn't
say anything about joining a monastery or abstaining from things that
give you pleasure. He, like other spiritual masters, enjoins us to bring
forth our truth and our gifts—you might do that by being a carpen-
ter, singing for children, raising a family, working the land, being the
CEO of a Fortune 500 company, or holding the intention that a moral
solution to a difficult problem in the workplace will be found. Furthermore, the right outlet for your gifts will shift throughout your life.
Radical activism might suit you for a number of years, and then you
may discover that being home with your young children is the best way
you can create the change you seek. You stop flying across the country
to walk in protest marches in Washington, but you now channel that
focus into teaching your children to be citizens of a global village. You
are still living out your calling, but you are expressing it in a new way.

Over time you might select a variety of 2% Projects. You will benefit
more and enjoy the harmony of your life more profoundly if you take
time to understand how each of these projects creates deeper meaning
in your life. Initially, as you are picking up and inspecting your life's
puzzle pieces, it may seem impossible that they will come together in
the spectacular way you desire. Yet harmony is the divine intention. Often the challenge is to avoid impeding the natural flow of universal energy. Saying yes to life is an act of courage which is richly rewarded.

Whenever I'm asked to give a short description of the 2% Solution,
I emphasize the harmony I see individuals experience when they give
2% of their time to that which really truly matters to them. I explain,
"When one makes that focused and disciplined commitment, then

everything else in his or her life flows better. It is a remarkable experience of alignment; all the other tasks, joys, and commitments in one's life begin to integrate." The 2% Solution leads to living an integral life—which is naturally a life worth living! Recognizing how to choose your path for higher meaning, if that calls to you, and how to integrate your four domains of self is our purpose in this chapter. The path is very much like a spiral; there's a long path with jigs and jogs as we become increasingly focused at our core.

The essential benefit is that the spiraling path keeps you centered and balanced according to the truths that resonate with your Esprit d'Core. As this happens, your core 2% reality begins to radiate with a power that can't be easily disrupted no matter what challenges come your way. It positions you in the tai chi stance with your feet shoulder width apart, your knees slightly bent, and your breath flowing. You have the strength and grace of a willow.

You will no longer worry about the possibility of living a fragmented life, because you will have developed calm internal trust and resonance. Of course, daily life will sometimes go in a hundred different directions, and you may feel fragmented at the outer level at times, but as your core strengthens, you will have new ways to respond to these challenges of external fragmentation by relying on your inner harmony. Your newly identified highest priorities will guide you.

THE INSISTENCE OF LIFE'S DEEP QUESTIONS

Some of us are moved to work with deep spiritual or existential issues because of an internal insistence; it is a quest that can only be fulfilled by answering the deepest questions of the heart. When this occurs, no superficial fix can possibly work; rather, we have to work with the deep questions of the meaning and purpose of life. Tolstoy graphically described this stage with striking awareness of his personal experience in his work titled *Confession* (1983, 26–27):

> *Five years ago something very strange began to happen to me. At first I began having moments of bewilderment, when*

my life would come to a halt, as if I did not know how to live or what to do; I would lose my presence of mind and fall into a state of depression. . . . Then the moments of bewilderment recurred more frequently, and they always took the same form. Whenever my life came to a halt, the questions would arise: Why? And what next?

At first I thought these were pointless and irrelevant questions. I thought that the answers to them were well known and that if I should ever want to resolve them, it would not be too hard for me. . .

I realized that this was not an incidental ailment but something very serious, and that if the same questions should continue to recur, I would have to answer them. And I tried to answer them. The questions seemed to be such foolish, simple, childish questions. But as soon as I laid my hands on them and tried to resolve them, I was immediately convinced, first of all, that they were not childish and foolish questions but the most vital and profound questions in life, and, secondly, that no matter how much I pondered them there was no way I could resolve them. . . . . In the middle of thinking about the fame that my works were bringing me I would say to myself, "Very well, you will be more famous than Gogol, Pushkin, Shakespeare, Moliere, more famous than all the writers in the world— so what?"

And I could find absolutely no reply.

When the shift in awareness becomes this strong, we *must* grapple with the meaning of life at the deepest personal level. It will be a full-bore inquiry into the meaning and purpose of whom and what we are. If you are wrestling with this intense questioning regarding the meaning of life, your 2% Solution may be to align with your sense of the divine and your spiritual purpose. The stunning depth of this challenge to your identity will require sustained support from all dimensions of your 2% Solution. Of necessity, you will be working on connecting this deeper sense of a transpersonal reality with how you are acting on this planet and your sense of higher purpose.

I boldly asserted in Chapter 4 the belief that identity rules. That is our personal sense of who we are governs our engagement with the world. Tolstoy's struggle is yet another example of the truth of the potency of this self-organizing principle. How we define ourselves has everything to do with our values, what we hold dear, and the challenges that feel most compelling to us. When a deep internal thrust insists that we address the deepest questions of the meaning of life, our sense of identity is certain to shift. It doesn't matter whether you are a bus driver, a teacher, a cook, or a senior VP; being on a path with heart and being of service are the true values.

SPIRITUALITY AND THE WORKPLACE

In my own research and that of others, it is clear that spirituality in the workplace is getting increasing play. World renowned business leadership advisor, Warren Bennis endorsed a collection of books devoted to inventive solutions which he considered new and exemplary contributions to management thought and practice. One of the most interesting is *A Spiritual Audit of Corporate America* (1999) by Ian Mitroff and Elizabeth Denton. In the Foreword, Bennis quotes one of my favorite books, *The Great Gatsby* by F. Scott Fitzgerald:

> Jay Gatsby…is standing at his favorite bar when the bartender says, "I hear you lost all your money in the stock market crash."
>
> "Yeah," Gatsby replies, "lost every last penny in the crash. . .but I lost all that was important to me in the boom."

Bennis relates Gatsby's losses to the epidemic of "affluenza" that has stricken the developed world—particularly the United States—in contrast with the values that authors Mitroff and Denton champion in taking on the question, "What is missing at work?" Bennis reports:

> *The heart of their argument is breathtakingly potent and it goes like this: Individuals and organizations that perceive themselves as "more spiritual" do better. They are more productive, creative, and adaptive. The people in these organizations are more energized and productive because work*

isn't solely about stock options and vacations and coffee breaks. Spiritual organizations are animated by meaning, by wholeness, and by seeing their work connected to events and people beyond themselves (xi–xii).

Mitroff and Denton report finding nearly unanimous agreement on the definition of spirituality and on the importance it plays in people's lives. The definition is simple and profoundly related to the purpose of the 2% Solution. "Spirituality is the basic desire to find ultimate meaning and purpose in one's life and to live an integrated life" (*xv*). They found that spirituality is often viewed in the workplace as an open topic related to meaning in life and work, to creativity, universality, and the positive expression of values, while religion is often viewed with words such as "narrow, prescriptive, dogmatic, restrictive, closed, exclusive, and so on" (40). If this is a central part of your 2% Solution, it is important for you to find creative, respectful ways to engage with others about your heart's focus.

SYNCHRONICITY

For months I had been mulling over creating a large emotional intelligence conference to expand the use of effective strategies for behavioral change in the workplace. At the end of an exhausting EQ conference in Florida, I ran into a woman I had wanted to connect with standing in the bookstore. She invited me to join her for a glass of wine, and within minutes I was telling her of my dream. She enthusiastically responded with creative thoughts and support. That first meeting mushroomed into a great collaboration—our symposium was held 10 months later and a friendship blossomed. We would both tell you it was simply meant to be!

A DEFINING MOMENT

Synchronicity refers to those magical moments when cause and effect just can't explain what happened. It's a connecting event between our psyches and an external event, in which we feel an unexplainable sense of inner and outer being linked. Instead of feeling ourselves to be separated and isolated, we feel a meaningful connection with others and the universe.

Synchronicity could be a significant factor in your 2% Solution. When you open yourself to wondering, learning, and growing, you invite connections that you could have completely missed otherwise. Additionally, one of your best allies in your process is likely to be the mysterious force which you might call the Universe, the Holy Spirit, a Higher Power, God, or Divine Intention. Whatever term works best for you, watch for synchronous opportunities. These gifts can be lost if you are unaware!

Synchronicity was a topic that fascinated the great Swiss psychiatrist and philosopher Carl Jung. In order to provide a more academic definition of the term, I turned to Jean Bolen, a well-known Jungian analyst. In her book *The Tao of Psychology* (1979, 6–7), she writes:

> *Jung described synchronicity as an acausal connecting principle that manifests itself through meaningful coincidences. There are no rational explanations for these situations in which a person has a thought, dream, or inner psychological state that coincides with an event. . . As a concept, synchronicity bridges East and West, philosophy and psychology, right brain and left. Synchronicity is the Tao of psychology, relating the individual to the totality. If we personally realize that synchronicity is at work in our lives, we feel connected, rather than isolated and estranged from others; we feel ourselves part of a divine, dynamic, interrelated universe.*

Bolen emphasizes that tuning into synchronicity can help us be aware of our intuitive wisdom and recognize that our lives have meaning. You will benefit by watching for clues in your life, and noticing what comes together for you on its own. Everything doesn't have to be hard! Watch for the gifts and ask any peers and mentors who are supporting you to join in the quest to notice and embrace the gifts of synchronicity as they enter into your life. As you observe these remarkable events happen in your life, your optimism and faith are likely to grow by leaps and bounds.

THE PATH OF SERVICE—BODHISATTVA

As you put into practice your 2% Project, I hope you will have a chance to experience the profound sense of the value that lies in being of service. Buddhists have a term for the ultimate in service which one human can perform—that model is called the *bodhisattva*. This refers to one who seeks the highest level of spiritual liberation in being a Buddha, but who commits to not take the final step in attaining enlightenment until he or she has helped all humanity reach the same level.

In taking the bodhisattva vow, the person commits to developing his or her own enlightened mind and to being of service to others. The enlightenment and service are in accordance with the six perfections of Buddhism: generosity, ethics, patience, effort, concentration, and wisdom. If you compare these to the strengths we discussed in Chapter 3, especially those which are based in the world's value systems, you will

> Do your work with the welfare of others always in your mind. By devotion to selfless work one attains the supreme goal of life.
>
> —*Bhagavad Gita*

find many parallels. We are much more similar to one another than different. As your 2% Solution takes you to valuing your community and exercising kindness, know you are making our world a better place.

PRACTICES

There are countless ways to implement your 2% Solution by following religious or spiritual paths. The few reviewed here are samples of the richness of possibility from which you might draw.

Affirmations, Positive Self-Talk

One strategy for expanding your connection with deeper meaning is to practice treating yourself well through your self-talk and by regularly affirming that your positive intentions have taken place. Too often our minds are fraught with judgmental and hurtful messages such as, "Dummy, why did you do that?" "Of course she got the award, she's so much smarter (better, faster, good looking) than I am." "I'm so slow and fat; why can't I just shape up?" I wouldn't be surprised if you could add a few from your own list in easily, as this is such a common behavior.

The fact that our culture is permeated with this kind of self-attack doesn't make it healthy. Not for a second. Give it up, if this happens to you. While I know this is easier said than done, you *can* develop a practice of treating yourself with the positive self-regard and love which the universe is continuously offering.

Use affirmations, or positive self-talk, to help yourself. Make a list of the most important intentions in your life, and then regularly and gratefully tell yourself out loud that these conditions already exist and are now going to be manifested in your outer life. Keep notes in your 2% Journal about your shifting self-image as you grow your compassion for yourself. Your earlier work with self-regard in Chapter 4 will provide additional support for this strategy.

Attitudinal Healing

In *To See Differently* (1990), Susan Trout wrote about the attitudinal healing process, which was founded on the thought system from *A Course in Miracles*. Jerry Jampolsky, the founder of the Center for Attitudinal Healing, created centers around the world that provide support for children who are dying of terminal illness. The work of the Center is to build community and learn how to choose love instead of fear.

Trout describes attitudinal healing as "working on one's own healing process and being of service to others. It is a way of life. . . It is about healing the mind so that one can live in this world with a sense of peace within and in relationships. It is about understanding the dynamics of the human psyche at both its conscious and unconscious levels. Above all, it is a way to care for one's emotional and spiritual well-being" (25). Attitudinal healing is another potent tool for self-development you could blend into the recipe of your 2% Project.

Physical Practices—Yoga and More

Many physical disciplines are designed to help you expand your connection with what is truly meaningful in the world. Yoga, tai chi, aikido, and qi quong are all examples of a process of movement that work with breath and the spirit to bring the body more fully to life.

By committing yourself to one of these or another physical practice on a regular basis, you will reap many benefits over time. Once the physical movements are mastered, the awareness shifts to the mind and spirit. As this occurs, a natural meditative state comes about.

A DEFINING MOMENT

Purpose fuels productivity. Practice moves us to Perfection. Patience is the heart of compassion.

Prayer, Worship

You might engage in prayer through your religious practices, such as saying the Rosary, or kneeling on your prayer rug toward Mecca six times a day. Or you may not have a religious affiliation, but you may have a strong connection with the divine and design your own prayer practice. Some people use the word *worship* to mean regularly attending services at their church, temple, synagogue, or mosque. However, a Native American prayer ceremony held in the sacred space of Nature with smudging and singing is an equally committed way to honor what is holy and sacred.

There are many ways to pray and worship to honor your spiritual or religious connection, to give that part of you a voice. The song that we came here to sing is most likely a joyful hymn of praise.

AA's 11th Step

Alcoholics Anonymous' Twelve-Step process can be a deeply spiritual journey. Some of the 2% in Motion stories throughout this book illustrate how some people used the 2% Process to work through their addictions. Many of those people included a spiritual component to their process. Addicts in these programs who are truly committed to freedom and life move through the 12 Steps very carefully, knowing that every day they are making a life-or-death decision. If they don't stay sober, if they drink or use, they will be dead or enter into a hell of guilt and self-torment that may be even worse. Many parts of the 12-Step process call for a connection with God, yet the practice is carefully centered "God as you know it to be."

Accordingly, for some it is a divine source they work with, for others it could be nature. Step 3 reads: "Made a decision to turn our will and our lives over to the care of God as we understood Him." Step 11 calls for action related to the topic of this chapter: "Sought through prayer and meditation to improve our conscious contact with God, as we understood Him, praying only for knowledge of His will for us and the power to carry that out."

One practice available for working the 11th step is a program offered through Contemplative Outreach. Several years ago my colleague Donald Masters worked with Father Thomas Keating to merge the 11th step with the practice of Centering Prayer. This training is now offered in several places throughout the United States. (More information is available in the Resources section at the end of the book.)

Meditation

Many choose a meditative or contemplative practice as a part of their 2% Process. Practitioners report benefits including enhanced peace of mind, a calmer demeanor, relief from stress and pain, reduction of anxiety, and much more. A report in the *Proceedings of the National Academy of Sciences* shows that the brain can be trained and modified through meditative practices (November 16, 2004). Researchers at the University of Wisconsin worked with Tibetan monks who had 10,000 to 50,000 hours of meditative practice and a control group with minimal training. Both groups were asked to meditate in a state of unconditional loving-kindness and compassion.

The neuroscientists found remarkable differences between the two groups. The researchers say the results suggest that the brain can be trained, as the brains of the long-term meditators showed more activity thar. those of the control group. Additionally, they report that the meditative practices affect the left prefrontal cortex, which is the part of the brain associated with having positive affective state. This finding is supported by discussions reported in 2003 with the Dalai Lama on how to work with the brain to create a more positive state (*Destructive Emotions*, 2003, by Daniel Goleman).

The conclusion has two critical components. First, the brain can be trained! The term used to refer to this process is *neuroplasticity* and it supports, among other factors, our discussion on emotional intelligence with more proof that you can grow your skills. Second, at least when done for significant amounts of time, meditation af-

> A musician must make music, an artist must paint, a poet must write if he is to be ultimately at peace with himself. What a man can be, he must be. He must be true to his own nature. This need we may call self-actualization.
>
> —Abraham Maslow

fects the part of the brain associated with our happiness. Here's some solid information on how to succeed in the pursuit of happiness—take this data and run with it!

Centering Prayer

The one meditation practice I'll mention in some detail is *centering prayer*. While it was developed by Catholic monks, its practice is nondenominational. It is a simple yet profound process, primarily asking the practitioner to spend 20 minutes in quiet, turning the time over to the divine twice a day. The suggestion is 40 minutes a day— not much different from the 30 minutes we've been talking about!

Father Thomas Keating is the well-known leader of the centering prayer movement and founder of Contemplative Outreach, which provides world-wide support for practitioners of this popular prayer practice. Their website aptly describes the history:

> *Centering Prayer is drawn from ancient prayer practices of the Christian contemplative heritage, notably the Fathers and Mothers of the Desert, Lectio Divina, (praying the scriptures), The Cloud of Unknowing, St. John of the Cross and St. Teresa of Avila. It was distilled into a simple method of prayer in the 1970's by three Trappist monks, Fr. William*

Meninger, Fr. Basil Pennington and Abbot Thomas Keating at the Trappist Abbey, St. Joseph's Abbey in Spencer, Massachusetts.

Keating's works, beginning with *Open Mind, Open Heart* in 1986, guide the reader to understand the psychological process that happens as we begin to engage in meditative practice. He writes that "one of the first effects of contemplative prayer is the release of the energies of the unconscious" (15). He explains these may show up as expressions of positive personal development or a humiliating awareness of our human weakness.

Anyone seriously engaged in deep personal growth can benefit from learning the basic descriptions he provides of the "False Self," which is a reflection of "our emotional programs for happiness." These programs developed through conditioning when we were children and, while more or less appropriate at the time, as adults they impede our ability to modify our behavior. Ultimately these old tapes are much of what we are wrestling with as we seek to be happier, more productive, and more authentic in our lives. How often have you found yourself looking for happiness in all the wrong places?

The emotional programs, as described in his later book *Invitation to Love* (1992), are (1) survival/security, (2) affection/esteem, and (3) power/control. He points out that these centers are instinctual needs which grow "into centers of motivation, around which our thoughts, feelings, and behavior gravitate." (145)

I've worked with centering prayer for years and had the joy of meeting with Father Thomas. This meditative practice is my primary 2% Project. Whatever the focus of your 2% Solution, if you are probing your thought system and behaviors to clear out old and limiting ways and making way for the new, you are likely to have to dance with your False Self and the emotional programs for happiness. Working with the concept of the False Self is another way of understanding your personal dragons and where they may lay.

2% in Motion

BE FRANK
Frank tells us "we are really neck deep in grace!" This wondrous soul worked as a manager of health, safety, and environment for

a building product manufacturer. His job has changed to include being a Six Sigma Master Black Belt. While this professional responsibility is important to Frank, he always puts it in context of his Soto-Zen meditation practice. Frank meditates at his home, participates in a spirituality group, and sits at the Sangha at Dragon Mountain in Crestone, Colorado where he has been accepted as a meditation partner.

Frank guides his life by wisdom sayings such as, "The wise man wants little, but nothing satisfies a fool." He says he'll know he has completed his 2% work when he wants less. Frank continually reminds himself that suffering is tied to impermanent things. He seeks to not get attached to the ups and downs of daily living and to "just let go and go for it!" Although he tries to be unattached, he is far from unengaged. Rather, he is fully engaged, while being unattached to specific outcomes. It can be a very difficult feat to be both fully committed and yet completely open to whatever happens along the way. I'm impressed with his commitment, and honor that he is a great example for all of us. %

Activity: *Selecting Your Practice*

To better understand the role spirit plays for you, identify three concepts that strongly call to you and contemplate them silently, then write your reflections down or talk with a friend about them. You might list ways that you can practice your preferences. Here are some possibilities:

Concepts/Values	Practices
• Strength	Affirmations, positive self-talk
• Courage	Attitudinal healing
• Character	Physical practices
• Moral fiber	Prayer, worship
• Determination	11th-step practice
• Chutzpah	Meditation

- Guts   Centering prayer
- Will   Meditation
- Force   Tai chi
- Heart   Centering prayer, affirmations
- Mettle   Affirmations, 11th-step practice

As you reflect, match the practices listed in the second column, or any others you feel attracted to, with the concepts that appeal to you. Notice how fully the possible practices listed—or others you may prefer—might help you implement the concepts or values that are most important for you. Then seriously consider undertaking one key practice to deepen your relationship with the divine or your greatest purpose. Take time to make this meaningful to you and bring it to life.

If you were to give your spirit more of the life energy that is currently employed in satisfying your emotional programs for happiness, how would you feel?

Engage Your EQ: *Self-Actualization*

While some think that self-actualization is an esoteric goal for the privileged few, research ranks it as universally essential to success. It is the first of the top five skills held by star performers in the workplace as identified by Stein and Book in *The EQ Edge*, and there is a lot at stake in learning this skill. According to Reuven Bar-On (2001), self-actualization requires both the ability and drive to set and achieve goals. Bar-On, author of the emotional intelligence inventory known as the EQi discussed in Chapter 1, believes that lifelong attention to these factors creates professional and personal success.

You can't bulldoze your way to self-actualization—it requires a balance of zest and rest, a harmony between passion and ecuilibrium. Mastering this balance yields a graceful life lived in passionate equilibrium. Therefore, I believe with all my heart that the challenges of the learning process will pay off for you.

Abraham Maslow began his research on self-actualization in 1935, as described in his seminal works, especially *Motivation and Personality* (1954) and *The Farther Reaches of Human Nature* (1976). His five-tier developmental process, which reflects the hierarchy we grow through as we build our capabilities and cope with our life conditions, is known as the *hierarchy of needs*.

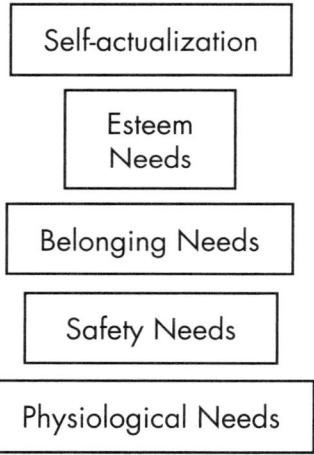

Humans have an inner drive to accomplish their purposes, and it is this energy and drive, this inner prod, which often leads to taking risky new steps. It helps us move out of the safe zones and grow. When we experience a feeling of discontent and restlessness, it is often because we are called to grow, painful and glorious though that may be.

Maslow identified two processes necessary for self-actualization: self-exploration and action. He insisted that the deeper the self-exploration, the closer one comes to self-actualization. I agree, and that is why I emphasize the reflective process so strongly. If we had to simplify the 2% Process and present only the bare-bone components, it would be to increase your self-reflection by taking time to explore and understand yourself, then to reflect with competent peers so you benefit from honest mirroring. The final step is to act!

Following the 2% Process will naturally promote your own self-actualization. Self-actualization is the EQ magnet that led many of the people I interviewed to change their lives so dramatically.

SELF-ACTUALIZATION: THE TOP-10 LIST

You are living a self-actualized life when you are motivated to set and achieve goals, when you know you are developing your potential, and when you are committed to bringing your gifts to fruition. This is truly about living a rich life. We gain the deepest sense of happiness and positive satisfaction when we are sharing our gifts most generously. This is the decisive factor in meeting the intention behind our theme poem and knowing for certain that we are singing our song! No doubt about it—if you know you're singing your song, you will have internal peace no matter how much external conflagration is going on around you.

Here are ten key points to remember about self-actualization:

1. Be willing to be your best self; embrace your gifts with passion!

2. Intend to be consciously self-aware; use the power of self reflection.

3. Pay attention to your inner wisdom; listen to yourself.

4. Listen with the ears of your heart to the reflections of others. If what they are saying speaks to you at the heart level, if you trust their insights, they are likely a qualified peer or mentor. Seek to understand their comments without creating a defensive shield.

5. Prioritize! This is a bedrock criterion for simplifying your life. You must make informed choices about how you spend your time and energy so you can focus on that which is most important.

6. Take risks. Too much safety can lead to mediocrity.

7. Focus on your principles; live in accordance with your personal mandate rather than public approval.

8. Accept responsibility; know that you are not a victim of the world you see.

9. Meditate, pray, create quiet contemplative time.

10. ACT!!

2% in Motion

ENJOYING THE BALANCE BEAM

After hearing me speak about the 2% Solution, Abbey sent me a letter eloquently explaining how her 2% Process sustained her through her challenging career in social services. She explained that she had worked for 30 years in a variety of capacities at a private agency, state hospital, and at the county department of human services. These positions were all in the same community and working with the same population of developmentally disabled children, adults, adolescents, and families in crisis. Despite these many years of service in the community, Abbey noted with some sadness that she knows few of her coworkers because of the high turnover. She wondered why she continued to stay when so many left so quickly.

Upon reflection, she attributed her staying power to her 2% Projects. She wrote:

"Your talk confirmed what I've known for a long time. Even though I've had extremely difficult work to do, I've managed to cope and not be consumed with the job due to totally disconnecting when the workday is over and doing fun things. One of my loves is music,

and I've taught piano and cello for many years. When I decided I wanted to start writing books and self-publish them a few years ago, I switched to that as my main project."

Your 2% Solution can support sustainability in the rest of your life as well as bringing great joy on its own. ◉

THE FOUR DOMAINS OF SELF

Living an integrated life is based on connecting our actions in the four domains of self— body, mind, heart, and soul. You may also see these domains referred to as physical, mental, emotional, and spiritual. Harmonious or resonant living emerges from integrating our activities and our attention in all four domains. It leads to fully experiencing the goals of authenticity, simplicity, and an integrated resonant life.

Of course, implementing this path doesn't mean that life will suddenly become all roses. However, as these skills become your reality, differences will occur. Also, recognize that you may experience the benefits internally while your outer world is still hectic.

While the four domains each need attention in your life, that does not mean you should expect that each one will receive equal amounts of time. Actually, it is highly unlikely. The right allocation depends on all the qualities that make up the unique person you are. The key point is to be certain you regularly check in with each domain; none should be ignored. You may have big opportunities in one domain that mean the other three are not as attended to for awhile. That is great if it reflects a valuable ebb and flow to your life. However, be especially careful that the disproportion isn't really an old habit in a new outfit.

You can create your own strategy for living an integrated lifestyle by incorporating the following exercise with the other work you have done through this book and in your 2% Journal. All your work has been oriented toward bringing your whole self fully to life. The game plan is created, and now you are taking the field and doing your warm-ups!

Activity: *Start Cross-training*

Design your cross-training strategy to spotlight your engagement in each of the four domains. A few examples are listed to get you started, but don't let them limit you—this is your list. Additionally, the examples are broad; you will gain the most by being much more specific. So instead of selecting exercise, write jogging or horseback riding, and so on for each category. Have fun discovering how many activities fit in more than one column—that is the magic of integration!

Body	Mind	Heart	Soul
Exercise	Learn	Connect	Meditate
Eat	Watch thoughts	Attitude	Pray
Relax	Read	Emote	Commune with nature
Renew	Solve puzzles	Tell the truth	Chant
Play	Make connections	Reach out	Dance
Heal	Heal	Heal	Heal
Cook	Compose	Sing	Sing
Sleep	Exercise	Forgive	Surrender
Reflect	Reflect	Reflect	Reflect

Record your cross-training plans in your 2% Journal.

Once you have designed your plan, live with it for a week. Then come back, check it out, and fine-tune it. Check in weekly, using your 2% Journal to gauge your success in executing your plan.

There are many methods and strategies that may contribute to your 2% Solution. In fact, it is fun to explore all of the options and with this in mind, I've included additional recommendations in the Resources section at the end of the book. Regardless of your choice of method, the benefits you seek only come through regular, sustained practice. It's the discipline you add that makes all the difference; you can have a great recipe, but without the action of mixing the ingredients together and baking the cake, you don't get to have dessert! This long-term, disciplined, and conscious implementation is the core of what it takes for you to reap the value from your 2% Solution and, certainly, it is the heart of living an integrated, rather than fragmented, life.

TUNE IN YOUR MIND

- Find the route to truth that is uniquely calling you and follow it through nature, spiritual practice, or religious observance.

- Explore the deepest mysteries in your life and discover unsuspected connections between meaning, feeling, and action in your life.

- Consider the bodhisattva path—as you seek and begin to regain your freedom and spiritual authority, share compassionately with others.

- Celebrate that you are becoming self-actualized—you are in the constant dance of becoming all you can be.

- Develop your integral practice with your four domains— body, mind, heart, and soul.

TUNE OUT THE NOISE

- Avoid any path that isn't founded in a heart calling.

- Don't let routine and daily hum-drum events eclipse the synchronicities and the larger patterns they reveal.

- Avoid following someone else's path. Listen to your internal guidance and find your own way.

....
A SNEAK PREVIEW

The Conclusion wishes you well on your journey and invites you to continue this life-altering practice.

CONCLUSION
Savoring Success and Serendipity

Now that you have digested this simple yet profound 2% Process, it's valuable to step back and remember the highlights. If, at this point in the book, you have your 2% Project fully engaged, consider hanging in there so it becomes a lifelong solution. If you are just now considering what project to undertake, get ready to launch.

Remember, your process will be unique to you. The 10-Step Action Plan will guide you through your journey, but it's not a linear process. You are the mapmaker, and who you are will change as you learn and grow. That's how you gain the marvelous benefits that otherwise might stay hidden just around the corner.

The 2% Process can be the perfect way to take time to answer the important philosophical questions that help you live at a deeper and more meaningful level. We benefit by applying well-defined processes when exploring such ancient questions as, "What am I here to do?" "How can I balance my life?" "How does my work fit into the larger picture of my life?" and "Am I fulfilling my life's mission?"

CHECK IN WITH YOUR AUTHENTIC SELF

Joseph Campbell left a profound legacy through his insightful guidance in understanding the human relationship with myth. Joining with Bill Moyers in their work entitled *The Power of Myth*, Campbell's powerful storytelling revealed to us a great deal about how we understand our world. He believed that what all human beings are most hungry for is true experience. He responded to a reflection by Moyers saying:

> "People say that what we're all seeking is a meaning for life. I don't think that's what we're really seeking; I think that what we're seeking is an experience of being alive, so that our life experiences on the purely physical plane will have resonances within our own innermost being and reality, so that we actually feel the rapture of being alive" (1988, 5).

Clearly, Campbell was on to something important. I describe the 2% Process as a way to connect meaning and action, which I believe is the same result that Campbell was espousing. We resonate with the innermost level of our being when we bring it to consciousness through the discipline of our 2% Project. This creates a direct, experiential event in our life in which our separate objective, individual sense of self gives way to an integrated experience of one whole self. We move out of our temporal frame of reference and slip into the flow of the timeless now.

A DEFINING MOMENT

The warning given by Socrates that the "unexamined life is not worth living" is not your problem! You are tackling the challenge he inscribed over the door of the Academy, "Know Thyself."

"Success" is a driving force for all our actions. We are motivated by the longing to achieve and that's okay. However, we will drive ourselves crazy seeking success if we don't tune in regularly to what matters most to us right now because our definition of success changes. Our focus on success is a gift if it is true, authentic success, not an external substitute created by the media. No fancy sports car, mansion, or amount of money indicates success. Consumption does not equal success!

Going for true success is so vital to achieving your 2% Solution that Chapter 3 addresses authentic success in detail. Look back at the Success Clarifier and the Success Quiz and note what you wrote about what success means to you. How are you applying the awareness you developed? Even better, now that you have so much more reflection and awareness under your belt, reapply the authentic success formula:

Authentic Success Isn't Really Algebra!

$$2\% + S + A + EQ = AS$$

2% of your time devoted to your 2% project + understanding and using your **strengths** + **awareness** of the relationship between your 2% Solution and your strengths + applying your **EQ** (emotional quotient), particularly your happiness and optimism, is guaranteed to = **Authentic Success**.

Are you who you say you are? Now that you have worked with your 2% Solution for awhile, and you have reviewed exercises which guided you to focus on what authentic success means for you, put your expanding skills in reflective awareness to work. Write about how authentic your success feels. Are there any parts that make you squirm or think "Well, but…?" Be completely honest with yourself; you deserve full candor. Are you creating the success that feels right at your core? If not, what action will you take? Reflect on these questions in your 2% Journal. What result did you get when you applied the authentic success equation? What can you applaud? Is there anything to fine-tune? Explore these questions as well in your 2% Journal now and periodically as a way to check in with your progress.

Be certain to give yourself *mega* credit for all your good intentions and your good work! Praise reinforces dedication, especially at the subconscious level—use it lavishly!

. . . .

RESONANCE

Resonare, meaning "to echo or resound," is the middle-French root word for *resonance*. The dictionary defines resonance largely in terms of vibrations and sound. When our daughter Julia brushes her teeth with her electric toothbrush, she hums in perfect pitch with the tune of this little machine. This is a classic example of resonance.

However, *Webster's Dictionary* also applies resonance to human behavior, defining it as "the complex of internal bodily processes that occur in emotional states [such as] rapport and empathy." Resonance is the state of feeling in harmony, released from nagging worries and free to be fully alive. It is reflected in a sense of wholeness, by heightened energy. When we're in resonance with our thoughts, feelings, and surroundings, we are open to synchronicity and savoring the great mystery.

In his inspirational autobiography *And There Was Light*, Jacques Lusseyran describes finding a barn as a boy at his grandparents' farm outside Paris in the early 1930s. Here he could relive the adventures of Robinson Crusoe, arrange logs to be a forest where he could set up armies and be Napoleon. Blinded at eight, he writes that "inside my body I had thousands of gestures which had been shut up there through the year in Paris, all the ones I had to make with careful calculation since I was blind" (1963, 47).

Freedom came for young Jacques from a space in which he could safely whirl, paddle, jump, skip, fall down, and get back up again. Can't you see him playing freely, exhilarating in the natural freedom of child's rambunctious play? This is resonance.

But how do we find resonance and why does it matter, anyway? It is easier to recognize rather than describe, because it unites our whole self in some unquestioned action. Spontaneity is a word that points to resonance. Spontaneous right action is a meaningful and gracious gesture that you make when you are doing something with such focused attention that there is no resistance. The self-doubts and "what ifs" drop away for a transparent moment in which you have disappeared into the event'space... and then—you're back.

When your life is humming in perfect pitch with the core of your being, it is because you are in resonance with the reason you are alive. If you pay attention to the delicately balanced conditions of opportunity and grace bestowed on you by life itself, you will be able to consciously experience the rapture of being alive.

Primal Leadership is an excellent book on integrating emotional intelligence into leadership development. Daniel Goleman, Richard Boyatzis, and Annie McKee begin their treatise by focusing on resonance and emphasize the value of leader and follower being on the same emotional wavelength. "A primal leadership dictum," they decree, "is that resonance amplifies and prolongs the emotional impact of leadership. The more resonant people are with each other, the less static are their interactions; resonance minimizes the noise in the system" (2002, 20).

Hence, being in resonance is a strong indicator of living authentically at work. The same principle applies at play and in prayer. When you are living in a way that echoes your deepest intention, your choices spring naturally from that internal source of wisdom, which is sometimes labeled the Divine, or God, or Oneness. Then you are in resonance; you are authentically engaged in life. This kind of living is integrated, not bifurcated. The promise of this huge gift is what invites you to integrate your whole self—body, mind, heart, and soul—to fully express your 2% Solution throughout your life.

Ultimately, every person is hungering to know how to hear the deepest guidance at their core and give expression to that wisdom. When we live our truth and take time to appreciate that this gift exists in each of us, whether we know it or not, we will not even wonder about authentic living; we will be humming along in unquestioned resonance with our well-lived life.

SAILING THE SPIRAL

Implementing your 2% Solution will have some ups and downs, as does any meaningful engagement. Your 2% Project is likely to reflect the zig-zag pattern of life. Have patience as you engage in this opportunity to bring your heart's calling to life. You are working at a deep core level when you strive to give up any lies you have been living with and relinquish loyalty to limitations that no longer need to restrict your life. It's fascinating how giving up once useful, even necessary, behaviors in order to actualize your evolving intention to thrive will bring you even more abundance.

This is a process of unraveling and outgrowing limiting beliefs and habits. As you do so, you will be sailing the spiral we've been discussing.

Synthesize your own personal set of tactics from the insights gathered from the models of Spiral Dynamics integral, Wilber's All Quadrant/All Level perspective, Cultural Creatives, and Father Keating's programs for happiness and teachings on the False Self. Develop your own individualized applications of these tools to the specific challenges you face. You are likely to distill a small set of techniques that work best for you. Master them, and stick with them for awhile.

Use the developmental systems that resonate with you, and let them inform you as you integrate your 2% Solution deeply into your life. Notice how your points of engagement with the world—friends, work, health, money, family, play—shift in strength and priority. Be aware of where you are currently being your highest self and write it down. If limiting beliefs or habits are causing a drag on your success, make a note of it in your 2% Journal and revisit your observations on a regular basis.

These tools are designed to facilitate deeper insight into yourself and a better understanding of other people and the world. By working with those that make the most sense to you and seeking to honestly understand what they reveal, you will excel in accomplishing your 2% Solution.

FINDING AND SUSTAINING 2% OF YOUR TIME

As you develop your 2% Project, you may find the rewards so powerful that you choose to keep it going. Somehow along the way your project may turn into a lifelong intervention, carrying you to the point from which you sing your song—that's your 2% Solution! Even if you don't specifically continue, you will gain many benefits. There will be many improvements in the quality of your life, probably the most significant of which will be the recognition that a small focused investment of your time can make such a valuable difference.

Throughout this book, I have told the stories of people who have been working with their 2% Solution, some for a decade and longer. Those who take their 2% Project to an extended application in their life reap the exponential benefits of wisdom and perspective. The path to this deeper and more mature engagement with life is illuminated by your 2% Solution.

"Great," you say. You'd love to continue this positive process, "but I'm worried that daily life will distract me. How do I sustain the momentum?" Excellent question! You are right; it isn't easy to consistently maintain a new behavior—that is, until it becomes a habit, the default response we always make unless there is an interruption. So the answer to sustaining your momentum while you change resides in your willingness to feel the internal pushes and the pain in your life, and to listen and learn. That willingness is often known as courage. Coupling this with your faith that you can succeed will produce the discipline it takes to sustain your effort.

The following strategies will help you in your daily practice of your 2% Solution. Remember that 30 minutes a day, or in clusters throughout the week, is your ticket to transformation. You can't force your way to authentic living—it requires a balance of zest and rest, a harmony between passion and equilibrium. Mastering this balance over time is what yields a graceful and exciting life.

- Engage with passionate equilibrium.

- Be consciously aware—pay attention to your choices. Reflect, reflect, reflect, individually and in groups.

- Set your intention for your 2% Solution and then pay attention to achieving it.

- Connect meaning and action deliberately and notice when you do.

- Say yes to conflict; embrace the teachings but don't dwell in the muck.

- Be patient; continuously remind yourself this is a journey.

- Embrace the positive.

- Use and continue developing your skills in emotional and social intelligence.

- Reward yourself for all you do which works well. Lavish abundant praise on yourself and others. Celebrate your 2% Solution.

- Be grateful!

EMBRACE THE FOUR BENEFITS

Secure your success by remembering to celebrate the four fabulous, life-changing benefits that come from implementing your 2% Solution that we discussed in the Introduction.

1. *Zest Appeal.* Live from the zest of Esprit d'Core; give your life the fullness and happiness that spontaneously flows from being committed to giving a voice to your inner wisdom.

2. *Congruency.* Align your values with your daily living and build up the true internal accountability, which creates authentic integrity.

3. *Identity.* Center on your internal truth to reveal your timeless identity so you don't lose your bearings when normal lifecycle losses come your way.

4. *Passionate Equilibrium.* Telling the truth—as hard as it is, sharing your joy—as big as it is—and being grateful for life exactly as it is will fuel you with the balance and grace that let you know you're living with passionate equilibrium.

BON VOYAGE!

It is with joy that I wish you a grand journey as you move forward in the field of rich rewards and great possibility. You will find my e-mail address in the Resources section at the back of the book. I would truly love to hear about your experiences in working with your 2% Solution. My final salutation is the Sanskrit blessing which means, "That which is resplendently divine in me salutes that which is resplendently divine in you!" *Namaste.*

RESOURCES

Contacting Marcia Hughes

Collaborative Growth helps people and organizations align their values and transform their results by integrating wisdom and passion, heart, and mind.

Marcia Hughes, President
Collaborative Growth
P.O. Box 17509
Golden, CO 80402
303-271-0021
contact@cgrowth.com
www.cgrowth.com
www.Lifes2PercentSolution.com

Assessments

You may contact me for information on the assessments discussed in this book by checking our website at *www.cgrowth.com*.

- The Bar-On EQi®
- The Bar-On EQ-360®
- Bar-On Leadership Report®

- Benchmarks of Emotional Intelligence
- Spiral Dynamics
- Emergenetics®

Other Referenced Resources

Influence and Focus leadership classes

These dynamic leadership programs run for nine months and focus on developing leaders from the inside out. That's the design and philosophy of both the ICAN *Influence* and ICAN *Focus* programs, which are hallmarks of the Institute for Career Advancement Needs (ICAN). The program leaders are Geil Browning, Carol Hunter, and Tim Rouse.

www.icanomaha.com/focus_influence/focus_home.html.

Spiral Dynamics integral

The primary site for Spiral Dynamics integral information is found at *www.spiraldynamics.net.*

You can find a full description of Spiral Dynamics with an active narrative on each of the eight levels at *www.wie.org/_flash/sd.asp*. Additional information, includes articles and resources by Don Beck.

www.humanemergence.org

Information on Spiral Dynamics and complementary tools is found at *www.5deep.net*

Integral Practice

Ken Wilber has created the Integral Institute, *www.integralinstitute.org*, and also has a website, *www.integralnaked.org*. Both have thoughtful, fun, and wildly diverse offerings to engage you in connecting with the four domains.

For additional information about Ken Wilber, see *wilber.shambhala.com.*

George Leonard and Michael Murphy are associated with the Esalen Center. Their book *The Life We Are Given* (1995) started a process which is now further established through their website, *www.itp-life. com*. They list groups in the United States and other nations through which members support one another in an integral transformative practice.

Cultural Creatives

http://www.culturalcreatives.org/

Emergenetics

www.cgrowth.com
www.emergenetics.com

Institute of HeartMath

Conducts research and supplies education on finding the balance between mind and heart in life's decisions. *www.heartmath.org*.

Happiness

Information on expanding your happiness is available at my website, *www.cgrowth.com*.

Martin Seligman's and his colleagues websites:

www.authentichappiness.org
www.reflectivehappiness.com

Research on positive psychology: *www.positivepsychology.org*.

An additional source is *www.worldlaughtertour.com*.

Spiritual References

Contemplative outreach and centering prayer:

www.contemplativeoutreach.org;

www.centeringprayer.com

11th-Step workshops

Contact Contemplative Outreach (*www.contemplativeoutreach.org*) or Madeline Soo at MLSOO@wi.rr.com.

Rabbi Rami Shapiro at One River Foundation for the Study of the World's Religions,

www.rabbirami.com.

12-Step Programs

This website is created and maintained by Alcoholics Anonymous World Services, Inc. The General Service Office is the international office serving AA in the United States and Canada. *www.alcoholics-anonymous.org.*

The 12 steps are listed at *www.recovery.org/aa/misc/12steps.html.*

REFERENCES

Auclair, Marcelle. 1988. *Saint Teresa of Avila*. Petersham, MA: St. Bede's Publications.

Bar-On, Reuven. 1997. *Bar-On Emotional Quotient Inventory Technical Manual*. Toronto: Multi-Health Systems, Inc.

_____ 2001. "EI and Self-Actualization." In *Emotional Intelligence in Everyday Life*, edited by J. Ciarrochi, J. Forgas, and J. Mayer. New York: Psychology Press.

Barks, Coleman. 1997. The *Essential Rumi*. Edison, NJ: Castle Books.

Barsade, Sigal, and Donald E. Gibson. 1998. "Group Emotion: A View from the Top and Bottom." In *Research on Managing Groups and Teams*, edited by D. Gruenfeld et al. Greenwich, CT: JAI Press.

Beck, Don, and Christopher Cowan. 1996. *Spiral Dynamics*. Oxford: Blackwell Publishers.

Bolen, Jean. 1979. *The Tao of Psychology*. New York: Harper and Row.

Borysenko, Joan. 1996. *A Woman's Book of Life*. New York: Riverhead Books.

Breen, Bill. 2000. "What's your Intuition?" *Fast Company*. September. 38.

Bridges, William. 1980. *Transitions: Making Sense of Life's Changes*. Reading, MA: Addison-Wesley.

Browning, Geil. 2006. *Emergenetics: Tap Into the New Science of Success*. New York: Collins.

Buckingham, Marcus, and Donald O. Clifton. 2001. *Now, Discover Your Strengths*. New York: Simon and Schuster.

Burns, David. 1980. *Feeling Good: The New Mood Therapy*. New York: Avon Books.

Butler-Bowdon, Tom. 2003. *50 Self-Help Classics*. London: Nicholas Brealey Publishing.

Cameron, Julia. 1992. *The Artist's Way*. New York: Tracher/Putnam.

Campbell, Joseph, and Bill Moyers. 1988. *The Power of Myth*. New York: Doubleday.

Childre, Doc, and Howard Martin. 1999. *The HeartMath Solution*. San Francisco: Harper.

Chopra, Deepak. 2004. *Book of Secrets*. New York: Harmony.

Collins, Jim. 2001. *Good to Great*. New York: Harper Business.

Contemplative Outreach. *www.centeringprayer.com*.

Cooper, Robert. 2001. *The Other 90%*. New York: Three Rivers Press.

Coffman, Curt and Gabriel Gonzalez-Molina. 2002. *Follow This Path*. New York: Warner Business Books.

Covey, Stephen. 2004. *The 8th Habit*. New York: Free Press.

_____. 1989. *The 7 Habits of Highly Effective People*. New York: Simon & Schuster.

Crum, Thomas. 1987. *The Magic of Conflict*. New York: Simon and Shuster.

Csikszentmihalyi, Mihaly. *1990. Flow*. New York: Harper and Row.

Dalai Lama (Tenzin Gyatso). 1990. *Freedom in Exile: The Autobiography of the Dalai Lama*. New York: HarperPerennial.

Dalai Lama (Tenzin Gyatso) and Howard C. Cutler. 1998. *The Art of Happiness*. New York: Riverhead Books.

de Graaf, John, David Wann, and Thomas H. Naylor. 2002. *Affluenza: The All-Consuming Epidemic*, Berrett-Koehler Publishers.

Dickinson, Emily. 1982. *Collected Poems of Emily Dickinson*. New York: Avenel Books.

Drucker, Peter. 2005. "Managing Oneself." *Harvard Business Review*, January, 100–109.

Editors. 2004. "Go with your Gut." *What Is Enlightenment*, May–July. Issue 25.

Ferguson, Marilyn. 1980. *The Aquarian Conspiracy*. Los Angeles: Tarcher.

Frankl, Viktor. 1959, 1992. *Man's Search for Meaning*. Boston: Beacon Press.

Gage, Fred. 2003. "Brain, Repair Yourself." *Scientific American*. September.

Goleman, Daniel. 2003. *Destructive Emotions: A Scientific Dialogue with the Dalai Lama*. New York: Bantam.

Goleman, Daniel, Richard Boyatzis, and Annie McKee. 2002. *Primal Leadership.* Boston: Harvard Business School Press.

Gowing, M.K. 2001. "Measurement of Individual Emotional Competence." *The Emotionally Intelligent Workplace*, edited by Cary Cherniss and Daniel Goleman. San Francisco: Jossey-Bass.

Gregg, Richard. 1936. *The Value of Voluntary Simplicity*. Wallingford, PA: Pendle Hill.

Hallowell, Edward. 2005. "Why Smart People Underperform." *Harvard Business Review*, January, 55–62.

Hobson, Allan J. 2000. *Consciousness*. New York: Scientific American Library.

Hoff, Benjamin. 1983. *The Tao of Pooh*. New York: Penguin.

Keating, Thomas. 1992. *Invitation to Love*. New York: Continuum.

____. 1986. *Open Mind, Open Heart*. New York: Amity House.

Kitayama, Shinobu, and Yukiko Uchida. 2003. *Journal of Experimental Social Psychology* 39, 476–482.

Klein, Gary. 2004. *The Power of Intuition*. New York: Currency Books.

____. 2000. "What's Your Intuition?" *Fast Company*. Issue 38:290.

Koch, R. 1998. *The 80/20 Principle: The Secret of Achieving More with Less*. London: Nicholas Brealey Publishing.

Kübler-Ross, Elisabeth. 1997. *On Death and Dying*. New York: Scribner.

Leonard, George, and Michael Murphy. 1995. *The Life We Are Given*. New York: Jeremy P. Tarcher/Putnam.

Lusseyran, Jacques. 1963. *And There Was Light*. New York: Parabola Books.

Lutz, A., L.L. Greischar, N.B. Rawlings, M. Ricard, and R. Davidson. 2004. "Long-term Meditators Self-induce High Amplitude Gamma Synchrony During Mental Practice." *Proceedings of the National Academy of Science (November 16)*, vol. 101, no. 46, 16369–16373.

Maharshi, Sri Ramana. 1972. *Be as You Are: The Teachings of Sri Ramana Maharshi*. Boston: Shambhala.

Maslow, Abraham H. 1976, 1993. *The Farther Reaches of Human Nature*. New York: Penguin.

_____ 1954, 1970. *Motivation and Personality*. New York: Harper Collins.

Mitroff, Ian, and Elizabeth Denton. 1999. *A Spiritual Audit of Corporate America*. San Francisco: Jossey-Bass.

Newberg, Andrew, Eugene D'Aquili, and Vince Rause. 2001. *Why God Won't Go Away*. New York: Ballantine Books.

Nichols, M.P., & Schwartz, R.C. (1991). *Family Therapy: Concepts and Methods*. Boston: Allyn and Bacon.

Pert, C. 2000. *Your Body is Your Subconscious Mind*. Boulder: Sounds True.

_____. 1997. *Molecules of Emotion*. New York: Simon & Shuster.

Potier, Beth. 2005. "HBS's Teresa Amabile 'tracks creativity in the wild'." *Harvard Gazette*, February. *www.news.harvard.edu/gazette/2005/02.10/09-amabile.html*

Ray, Paul, and Sherry Ruth Anderson. 2000. *The Cultural Creatives*. New York: Harmony Books.

Rilke, Rainer Maria. 1984. *Letters to a Young Poet*. Translated by Stephen Mitchell. New York: Random House.

Russell, Peter. 1998. *Waking Up in Time*. Novato, CA: Origin Press.

Schachter-Shalomi, Rabbi Zalman. 1997. *From Age-ing to Sage-ing*. New York: Warner Books.

Seligman, M. 2002. *Authentic Happiness*. New York: Free Press.

Sheldon, Kennon, Andrew Elliot, Youngmee Kim, and Tim Kasser. "What is Satisfying about satisfying events?" *Journal of Personality and Social Psychology*, Feb. 2001: 325–339.

Simon, Scott, John de Graaf, David Wann, and Thomas Naylor. 2001. *Affluenza: The All-Consuming Epidemic*. San Francisco: Berrett-Koehler.

Spiral Dynamics. *www.spiraldynamics.net*.

Stein, Steven, and Howard E. Book. 2000. *The EQ Edge: Emotional Intelligence and Your Success*. Toronto: MHS.

Stein, Steven. 2002. "The EQ Factor: Does Emotional Intelligence Make You a Better CEO?" *MHS*, November. *www.emotionalintelligencemhs.com/EQFactor.asp*

Stix, Gary. "Ultimate Self-Improvement," *Scientific American*, September 2003, 45

Tolle, Eckhart. 1997. *The Power of Now*. Novato, CA: New World Library.

Tolstoy, Leo. 1983, 1996. *Confession*. Translated by David Patterson. New York: Norton.

Trout, Susan. 1990. *To See Differently*. Washington, DC: Three Roses Press.

Wallis, Claudia. 2005. "The New Science of Happiness." *Time Magazine Special Edition: The Science of Happiness*. January 17.

Whalen, E. 1995. Foreword in *Power vs. Force* by David Hawkins. Carlsbad, CA: Hay House.

Wheatley, Margaret. 1992. *Science and the New Leadership*. San Francisco: Berrett-Koehler Publishers.

Wilber, Ken. 2000. *A Theory of Everything*. Boston: Shambhala.

_____ 1995. *Sex, Ecology, Spirituality*. Boston: Shambhala.

_____ 1991. *Grace and Grit: Spirituality and Healing in the Life and Death of Treya* Boston: Shambhala.

Wilhelm, R., and C. Baynes. 1981. *The I Ching* (3rd ed. Translation from Chinese). Princeton, NJ: Princeton University Press.

ABOUT THE AUTHOR

Marcia Hughes is president of Collaborative Growth, LLC, and devotes her life to guiding clients and colleagues to bringing their life's purpose to the forefront. She is co-author of *Emotional Intelligence in Action* (Pfeiffer, 2005), a professional speaker, and serves as a strategic communications partner for leaders and teams in organizations that value high performers. She weaves her expertise in emotional intelligence throughout her consulting work to help people motivate themselves and communicate more effectively with others. Her keynotes are built around powerful stories of how success can grow when people work collaboratively and when individuals "sing their song." Businesses, governmental agencies, and nonprofits have all benefited in such areas as leadership and team development, strategic design, and conflict resolution from her proven formula for success. Marcia offers keynotes and workshops on Life's 2% Solution.

Marcia is a certified trainer in the Bar-On EQ-i and EQ-360. She certifies senior human resources leaders, coaches, and consultants to utilize these measures with the people they lead. She provides Train the Trainer training and coaching in powerful EQ delivery. Her inspiration and persistent efforts led the development, promotion, and hosting of Collaborative Growth's International EQ Symposium in 2004, which attracted participants from nine nations. It focused on distilling effective strategies for behavioral change from the theory and research on emotional intelligence. She and her team are actively developing the 2006 Symposium.

Her efforts to improve productivity in the workplace through strategic communications grew out of a distinguished career in law, where her firm specialized in complex public policy matters. There again, her leadership and communication skills enabled Marcia's team to effectively address controversial environmental, land use, and water development matters involving numerous stakeholders, which included federal, state, and local governments along with the general public.

As an Assistant Attorney General she served the Department of Public Health and the Environment, she clerked on the 10th Circuit Court of Appeals for the Honorable William E. Doyle and served with the Environmental Protection Agency in Washington, D.C.

INDEX